More Stories from Ontario's Most Dangerous City

From Beyond The Yellow Tape

Thank you and enjoy reading

RICK DIGIANDOMENICO

More Stories from Ontario's Most Dangerous City
From Beyond The Yellow Tape

Copyright © 2023 by Rick DiGiandomenico

All rights reserved.

ISBN: 9798844614682

KDP Independent Publishing Platform

No part of this book may be used or reproduced by any means, graphic, electronic or mechanical, including photocopying, recording, taping or by any information storage and retrieval system without the written permission of the publisher except in the case of brief quotations embodied in critical articles and reviews.

DEDICATION

For the men and women in law enforcement who put their lives on the line daily for our safety and for their families who support them. To the memory of all the police officers who gave their lives in the line of duty.

To my loving wife, Rose. Thank you for your patience and love which allowed me to do something I loved. I am grateful. To our precious and beautiful family including our three children, our daughter-in-law, two sons-in-law and two grandsons.

TABLE OF CONTENTS

	DEDICATION	iii
	ACKNOWLEDGEMENTS	vii
	PROLOGUE	9
1	The Covid Years	11
2	How's The Old Ticker Doing?	19
3	Grandma And The Bungling Burglars	26
4	Before You Go See The Priest, Leave Your Gun At Home	33
5	Death Stinks	40
6	The Carnival Comes To Town	49
7	Hit and Run	53
8	The Mundane Parts Of The Job	59
9	There Will Always Be At Least One Gun There When You Arrive At The Scene	77
10	Pyjamas And A Deck Of Cards	86
11	Failure In More Ways Than One	97
12	Is That A Gun In Your Pants, Or Are You Just Happy To See Me?	105
13	Nothing Like A Sunday Afternoon Brawl	111
14	Batman Needs Assistance	116

15	One Fatal Night	124
16	Can't Get Enough Of Those B&E's	131
17	Watch out for flying beer bottles	142
18	Is It The Heimlich Or The Hind-Lick Manoeuvre	148
19	Like Something You Would See On TV Or In A Movie	154
20	One Of My Last Investigations Before Retirement	161
21	One Child's Horrific Memories	169
22	Murders in South Simcoe	176
23	The Night Shift	181
24	Not-So-Honorable Mentions	188
	EPILOGUE	194

ACKNOWLEDGMENTS

For privacy purposes I have omitted certain names and have changed the names of certain individuals to disguise their identities. This was done to protect the innocent (and the stupid). I have also changed some of the street names or locations pertaining to specific incidents that I wrote about. The views and opinions expressed in this book are mine alone and do not necessarily reflect those of any specific police service.

As in my first book, the incidents that I write about are based on information obtained from incident reports, police notebooks, newspaper articles and from my own personal recollection of what occurred during these investigations and follow-up investigations conducted by myself and other officers. I've said it before, and I'll say it again. When it comes to personal memory or recollection, there are some things that you will never forget. Some of these stories that you are about to read will be forever ingrained in my mind.

PROLOGUE

I invite you once again to join me for some additional stories from *Ontario's Most Dangerous City*. At least that's what Brantford was being called back in 2008. Brantford was designated as the eleventh most dangerous city in Canada and the crime capital of Ontario between 2006 and 2008. You don't have to take my word for it. Check out the *2008 Maclean's National Crime Rankings*.

After writing and self publishing my first book, I didn't really believe that I would be writing a second one. I knew that I had enough stories for a second book but didn't feel as though my heart was into it. Why bother? But then I started hearing from friends and family. They encouraged me to write another book. *"When are you going to write your next book?" "I can't wait to read your next book."*

So after more than five years later, here it is. The stories that I write about are pretty well every day situations that police officers get involved in. It gives you a glimpse of insight into what it's like to be a police officer. You have to be there to experience what it's really like. The sights, sounds and smells of the environment that you are in. The adrenaline rush pumping through your veins. Adrenaline is also known as the "fight or flight" hormone. It's released in response to a stressful, exciting, dangerous, or threatening situation. Watching this type of excitement on a television screen or reading about it in a book is probably the next best thing to actually being there.

While writing my first book, I found it to be very therapeutic for me. Some of these incidents that I wrote about brought back both good and bad memories. Putting them in writing has helped me to not only reminisce about my career but it has also allowed me to find some closure. This time around, I left out any stories involving office politics. When negative office politics begin to fester in the workplace, your organization can suffer. That's the only comment I will make in this book regarding this toxic subject.

CHAPTER ONE

The COVID Years

I know that you are tired of hearing about the COVID pandemic. Well, you are going to be reading about it in the following pages of this chapter. Or, you can choose to skip this part of the book and move on to the next chapter. Apparently, there are several common words and phrases surrounding the pandemic that people got tired of hearing. Words and phrases that we never want to hear again. These include, *"the new normal," "social distancing," "unprecedented times," "we're in this together," "out of an abundance of caution," "supply-chain issue," "flattening the curve," "wash your hands"* and the only time I ever want to hear about a *"facemask"* is during an NFL game. As long as the penalty is being called on the opposing team. Anyway, I will try my hardest not to use any of these above words or phrases in this book.

I don't have to tell you how difficult the last few years have been. I remember when I was concerned about some money investments that were made in early 2020. I was on the phone talking to a financial advisor at the bank. We were discussing this new infection or disease called the coronavirus which was later renamed COVID-19. At first, all we knew was that this virus was spreading around the world causing respiratory illness, pneumonia, and death. I told the advisor that I was concerned because our mutual fund investment had tanked and the value was dropping quite a bit. There was talk about an impending province wide lockdown to prevent the spread of this dreadful disease. I am now going to paraphrase what the guy at the bank told me.

"Hey Rick, I wouldn't worry about the investments. They're making a mountain out of a mole hill. I just heard on the news that there are three confirmed cases in Toronto and the media is acting like there's an Ebola outbreak. It's only three people out of the entire population of Toronto, for Christ's sake! It'll blow over before you know it. Like I said, don't worry about it. And that possible lockdown that they're talking about on the news? That's bullshit. It'll never happen."

Well, thank you so much for that wonderful piece of advice. How did that turn out? As we all know, the shutdown finally came on March 17, 2020. We all thought it was going to last maybe a couple of weeks and finally things would get back to normal. Right?

Unfortunately, we lost our dear mother, Domenica on March 25, 2020. Mom passed away in her 85th year due to complications from pneumonia. This was just eight days after we went into lockdown. There was no visitation allowed and attendance at all funeral services was restricted to a maximum of ten people due to government restrictions. The ceremony was held at the funeral home chapel since churches and all places of worship were forced to close during the pandemic lockdown. The whole situation was surreal. There were only ten people allowed at the interment. We gathered inside the mausoleum with the casket. The priest read a verse of scripture, said a special prayer and delivered a blessing. Although we wore masks, we were not allowed to view the actual interment or entombment which usually takes place in more confined spaces. We were not pleased about this but there was no use in complaining to anyone. It was beyond our control. It was the beginning of the COVID nightmare.

During the summer of 2019, we had to place our mother in a long-term care facility. We tried to keep her at home for as long as possible but it just didn't work out. She was unable to take care of herself due to deteriorating health. We helped out as much as possible and did the best we could. There comes a time when you have to be honest with yourself and decide on the best course of action. A higher level of care provides both increased safety and comfort for an aging or ill loved one. Moving your elderly parent into assisted living might be one of the hardest decisions you'll have to make in your life. We had no other choice and we did what we had to do.

    Afterwards, we ended up having to declutter mom's home and put it up for sale. It was a very unpleasant and difficult experience. It was quite an ordeal having to sort through all of our mother's possessions. Going through all of the household items brought back many nostalgic memories for both my sister and I. This was the house that my parents lived in for fifty-three years. It was the home that we grew up in. Now we had to make snap decisions about what to keep, toss, sell, give to family members or donate to charity. I wish that our mom could have taken part in this process so that she would have been able to get some closure.

    My father, Lorenzo had been living in a long-term care facility when he passed away in his 83rd year, on April 28, 2010. That was way before COVID-19. He had been officially diagnosed with Alzheimer's in 2006 and slowly slipped away from us. That was definitely a hard time for our family. Anyone who has ever had a family member diagnosed with dementia or Alzheimer's knows exactly what I'm talking about. My dad died in April, 2010 but we really lost him in 2006 when his mind had deteriorated and he completely shutdown mentally and physically. He was also confined to a wheelchair.

Now getting back to the pandemic. On December 18, 2020 Rose and I sent an email to our three children and their spouses. It was probably one of the hardest things that I have ever had to do. The following is the exact wording of the email that was sent.

Hi kids,

As you probably already know, Premier Doug Ford will be making an important announcement this coming Monday. Sounds like more lockdowns are in the works. Hamilton is going into lockdown starting on Monday. The fact that this is all happening just before Christmas is no coincidence. Brantford-Brant County will be moving into the RED Zone starting on Monday as well. This means that only five people will be allowed to gather indoors. They are strongly encouraging people to limit social gatherings to only include members of the same household.

As we continue to hear about the increasing numbers of COVID-19 cases and hospitalizations, we have become more and more concerned about our health and getting together this Christmas. We want everyone to stay safe and healthy as we approach the New Year. We have exciting things happening in 2021 along with more holidays and celebrations to look forward to. For all of these reasons, Mom and I have had to make a very difficult decision to cancel our family gathering for Christmas this year.

Instead, we will be celebrating Christmas with just the two of us and Marley, of course. We hope that we will be able to Zoom with you

kids or call each other on Christmas. That would be nice. Thank you for understanding and we'll talk soon. XOXO
Love, Mom and Dad

What a crazy time it was. Never in my wildest dreams could I have imagined that I would end up cancelling our family Christmas get-together. I had celebrated this wonderful day of the year with family members for sixty-two years of my life. And yet, this was the email that we sent just a week before this blessed celebration.

My daughter Jennifer initially thought that this was some kind of a sick joke and was waiting for the punch line. Anybody who knows me, can tell you that I enjoy kidding around and being sarcastic. Not this time. I was serious. Deadly serious. She later responded to my email after realizing that this was not a joke. This was her reply:

Okay, the shock of our Christmas gathering being cancelled has worn off! Lol. Just wanted to say that I totally respect your decision and am glad you are being cautious. I'm sure it was a difficult decision for you guys to make.

All of our children felt the same way and respected our decision. However, we were able to compromise a little bit. We definitely did not have our usual family gathering but we did manage to do a few smaller, individual visits. But it sure wasn't the same. We had separate visits with our kids so that we could exchange Christmas gifts. The visits were short and sweet but nothing like our usual festivities. This was life back in 2020.

Mark and Trisha visiting us for Christmas during COVID – Dec. 24, 2020
"Baby, It's Cold Outside"

In March of 2021, while still in the grips and throes of the COVID pandemic, we lost our precious Golden Retriever, Marley. He was a gentle and loyal companion. He was loved by everyone and this was another big loss for us. He was thirteen years old when he died peacefully at home, surrounded by his family. During the past several weeks before he passed, we began to notice a decline in his mobility which deteriorated to the point where he was unable to lift himself up, lay down or walk on his own. It was time to put Marley to sleep. He was made to feel as comfortable as possible without any pain. Our kids came over that weekend so that they could be with him for the last time. Our son, Mark, drove all the way from his home in

Ottawa to see Marley. We will remember him as a lively and joyful dog. He brought us much happiness over the years. Some people may find it strange to hear someone talking about an animal as if they were human. Anyone who has ever had a pet for a long time can understand and appreciate our feelings. They truly become part of the family and are missed when they are gone.

In April of 2022, my wife Rose and I both tested positive for COVID-19. At the time, we were triple-vaccinated and our symptoms were relatively mild. They included a sore throat, headaches, sneezing, runny nose, coughing, feeling tired and run down. It felt like a bad cold or the flu. The worst part was that I was unable to taste or smell my food for awhile. We isolated at home and rested up until we began to feel better about a week later. There's really not much else I can say about COVID. You know how the story goes unless you've been living under a rock for the last few years. So, I'll just leave at that. Enough said.

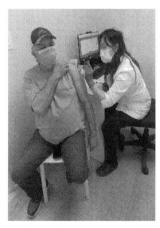

Getting my first COVID-19 vaccine

CHAPTER TWO

How's The Old Ticker Doing?

I had finally published my first book in April of 2017 and was feeling pretty good about it. I wanted to be able to share my stories and offer some insight on my experiences. Kind of like an autobiography and memoir rolled up into one. These stories might make people more vigilant and help to enhance safety awareness. As the old saying goes, *"even if I can help one person then I feel as though I have done some good."* Or something like that.

About two months after publishing I was starting to feel unwell. Sometimes I would experience tightness in the chest, shortness of breath, heart palpitations and some coughing. On one particular evening, Rose drove me to the hospital emergency department where I had some x-rays done. I was told by the emergency room doctor that I would need some further testing. The doctor had seen something in the x-ray images that didn't look right. They booked me in for a CT scan the following day. Within a couple days, I received a phone call from my family doctor. I was told that the CT scan showed an ascending aortic aneurysm.

It was explained to me that this type of aneurysm consists of a bulge in the wall of the aorta, the main artery from your heart. Aortic aneurysms form in a weak area in the artery wall. They may rupture (burst) or split (dissect), which can cause life-threatening internal bleeding or block the flow of blood from your heart to various organs. Canadian actor, Alan Thicke's death was caused by an acute aortic dissection. This is the same cause of death that led to the tragic loss of life of fellow Hollywood comedian and actor, John Ritter who starred in the television series, Three's Company. So what now?

After consulting with a Hamilton heart surgeon, it was decided that I needed to go in for open heart surgery in order to repair the aortic aneurysm. During a coronary angiogram, it was also discovered that I had two blocked arteries that would require bypass surgery. I asked the surgeon if I would be able to postpone the surgery until after my daughter's wedding. He looked at me straight in the eye and said, *"Rick, you might not make it to the wedding day. You need to have it done as soon as possible."* I was stunned to hear this and it was at this point that I realized how serious my condition was. My brain needed time to digest all this information that I had been given. Thankfully, all went well and I was able to walk Jennifer down the isle on her wedding day. And of course, that was followed by the weddings of our two other children. I appreciate how fragile life can be and how important it is to take care of ourselves. We owe it not only to ourselves but to our loving families as well.

On the other hand, some of the best-selling authors today have one thing in common: they are all dead. Musicians who die unexpectedly see their album sales boosted by a combination of nostalgia and curiosity. Many artists experience their biggest sales after death. Do you see where I'm going with this train of thought? I published in April, 2017 and my open heart surgery was scheduled for October, 2017. So I thought, heaven forbid I should be met with an untimely death. Just think about the spike in book sales. Okay, maybe not. I know….I know. This is not something to joke about, especially when you consider the unfortunate people who have died on the operating table. This is what we call dark or gallows humour and most cops subscribe to this type of humour. It's how we deal with things. Get over it. Anyway, all went well with my surgery and I was able to recover very nicely at home. As a result, I have been able to write my second book. If you don't like this book, you can blame my heart surgeon.

On a final note, many people ignore the warning signs of a heart attack or wait until their symptoms become unbearable before seeking medical help. Others wait until they are absolutely sure it's a heart attack because they worry they will look foolish if it is a false alarm. These reactions can result in dangerous delays. Don't be one of these people.

Pay attention to your body and call 911 if you experience:

- *Chest discomfort. Most heart attacks involve discomfort in the centre of the chest that lasts more than a few minutes – or it may go away and then return. It can feel like uncomfortable pressure, squeezing, fullness or pain.*
- *Discomfort in other areas of the upper body. Symptoms can include pain or discomfort in one or both arms, the back, neck, jaw or stomach.*
- *Shortness of breath. This can occur with or without chest discomfort.*
- *Other signs. Other possible signs include breaking out in a cold sweat, nausea or feeling lightheaded.*

On a happier note, some really great things have happened since I published my first book. You see, it's not all gloom and doom. As I mentioned earlier, all of my three children got married. Jennifer married Christopher in May, 2018. The wedding celebration took place at the historic Arlington Hotel located in the picturesque downtown Paris,

Ontario (the prettiest little town in Canada). That wonderful day began and ended amid a stunning riverfront scenery. Jenn and Chris now have two children named Zachary (Zack) and Maksym (Maks). Zack was born in February, 2019. Maks was born in September, 2022. Yup, that's right. Rose and I are now grandparents. And loving it!

Christine married Bradd in August, 2020 and Mark married Trisha in August, 2021. As you can see, two of the weddings took place during COVID. All necessary precautions were taken and public health measures and restrictions were adhered to. A great time was had by all. Christine and Bradd's wedding celebration took place at the Hamilton Golf and Country Club. It is one of the oldest and most prestigious clubs in the country. The venue is located in Ancaster and is nestled atop the Niagara Escarpment. The property includes a historic clubhouse along with beautiful gardens. We also enjoyed a fabulous outdoor patio space that overlooks the spectacular finishing hole of the Canadian Open.

Our final matrimonial event took place at a beautiful place known as Compass Rose. It is located in the heart of Prince Edward County. This is where Mark and Trisha were married. The ceremony took place at an outdoor site surrounded by many acres of fields and forests. It's an awesome venue that includes a variety of ceremony sites, glass greenhouse, giant fire pit, rustic barn and an elegant farmhouse with on-site accommodation. Each of these weddings were such a joyous and wonderful occasion for us. We would have loved to have had more extended family and friends attend the wedding celebrations. Unfortunately, this was not possible due to the pandemic restrictions on gatherings. However, we felt blessed knowing that those who could not join us, were definitely with us in love and in spirit. We also appreciated everyone's understanding and support. Rose and I are grateful to have our adult children, their spouses and grandchildren in our lives.

We also downsized from our two-storey home, that we lived in for thirty-five years. We purchased a new build condominium in Paris, Ontario. No more yard work or shovelling snow. Construction of the condo building began in October, 2019 (just before COVID-19 reared its ugly head) and we finally moved into our new home in February, 2022. During construction, there were a lot of delays and disruptions caused by the pandemic. Needless to say, we have been quite busy in the past few years. I could probably fill a book based on everything that's happened during that particular time period.

Located just a few kilometers northwest of Brantford, Paris is a beautiful small town that is filled with attractions, activities, and places to visit. When I first came to this area in 1985, the population of Paris was around seven thousand. Now it's fifteen thousand people and still growing. Many new homes continue to be built in this area. The town is set between the Grand and Nith Rivers. There are plenty of trails to explore by biking or walking. The two rivers are perfect for some paddling by canoe or kayak. There's also a beautiful park nearby. Rose and I truly enjoy living here. However, if Paris gets too big for us, we'll have to find a smaller town to move to. Just kidding!

There you have it. I've given you a bit of an update on my family and personal life. A lot has happened since I wrote and published my first book. I don't use any social media such as Facebook, Twitter or Instagram. This is how most people keep in touch with each other to provide life updates. Instead, I thought I would devote a few pages of my books and write about some personal experiences for anyone who might be interested. If you're not, that's okay. Now I would like to move on to some policing stories and anecdotes from days gone by.

CHAPTER THREE

Grandma And The Bungling Burglars

I was on patrol one night in March of 1988 when I got dispatched to a residential Break and Enter in progress (B&E). This type of call means that one or more burglars may still be inside the residence as police respond to the scene. An elderly woman, in her eighties, called the Brantford Police to report that she was in her upstairs bedroom and could hear someone moving around inside her home. She believed that an intruder was trying to get into the bedroom and that she had seen the door knob being turned. The two-storey house was located on Dundas Street near Wells Avenue.

It was sometime after 10 p.m. when I got the call and Police Officer Mark along with an auxiliary officer were also dispatched to back me up. I responded to the call with lights and siren. I was concerned that if there were any intruders inside the house, their actions could potentially escalate, leading them to cause harm to the homeowner or take her hostage. I shut off the siren when I was a few blocks away and parked my cruiser a couple of houses down from the incident location. I didn't want to give the bad guys a heads up on my arrival. I approached the residence on foot and started checking the doors and windows. I went to the back of the house and noticed that a basement window was broken. I advised the dispatcher that entry had been gained through a basement window located at the rear of the residence. I then heard the police cruiser pull up with Officer Mark and the auxiliary officer. I told Mark to watch the front of the house while I covered the back.

    All of a sudden, I heard some glass breaking and looked up towards the second floor of the house. An upstairs window glass and frame had been smashed out and fallen to the ground in the backyard. I observed a male suspect standing in front of the broken window. He had kicked out the window and was just about ready to jump out but changed his mind when he realized that I had seen him. Now he had to come up with a plan B. He began yelling and shouting but I couldn't make out what he was saying. Maybe he was trying to warn his buddy or he might have been yelling obscenities at me for having thwarted his escape attempt. He suddenly disappeared from my sight and I didn't know where he had gone to at this point. I yelled over to Mark to alert him as to what had just happened.

We now had confirmation that this was definitely a break and enter in progress with one or more suspects inside. I updated the dispatcher and advised that we were going into the residence. Additional units were dispatched to assist. We unholstered our firearms and approached the rear porch of the house. We stepped onto the porch and observed that the door was ajar. We slowly pushed it open so that we could make entry. As the door opened, we found two male suspects standing in the kitchen like deer caught in the headlights.

These two schmucks finally realized that they had reached the end of the road and that there was no where for them to run. I yelled, *"Police, don't move!"* I pointed my revolver directly towards the suspects and ordered them to the ground. *"Get on the ground! Get on the fucking ground right now and don't move!"* They laid face down with their arms outstretched in front of them. I handcuffed one of the suspects while Mark handcuffed the second guy. Apparently, they had unlocked the back door and were getting ready to make a run for it, just seconds before we interrupted their escape plan. I guess that was their plan B.

After they were handcuffed, we escorted them to Mark's cruiser and searched both suspects prior to putting them in the back seat of the police car. During the search of our prisoners, we found and seized two knives and a small plastic bag containing a quantity of marijuana. Mark and the auxiliary officer transported both prisoners to the station for processing along with the seized items.

    I went back into the residence to make sure that the burglary victim was safe and that she wasn't injured. She was a little shaken but otherwise she was doing just fine and thanked us for helping her. She said that she was extremely happy and relieved to see us. We removed her to a safe area so that I could go in with other officers to search and clear the rest of the house. This was done to make sure that there were no other intruders in the home that may have been hiding somewhere. We cleared the home and did not find anyone else inside.

    Detective Ken arrived on scene and took a statement from the break-in victim. She told the detective that she held her bedroom door shut against the intruders until police arrived. She was a brave woman to be able to do what she did. She remained calm throughout the ordeal. I found out later that when she saw the bedroom door knob turning, she yelled out, *"Whose there? Get out of my house! I've called the police and they're on their way!"* We have to remember that the homeowner was in her eighties at the time of this incident. Way to go Grandma!

One of the culprits was twenty-two years old and his partner in crime was twenty years old. Both of them were under the influence of alcohol and drugs at the time of this incident. The 20-year-old had prior convictions for breaking and entering. He had recently been arrested for breaking into a Chinese restaurant. He was sentenced to six months in jail after he pleaded guilty to charges of breaking into the restaurant and breaking into the Dundas Street home. At the restaurant, a television, stereo and beer were stolen. I don't know what happened to the 22-year-old but I'm guessing that he also plead guilty and received some jail time. I never received a trial notification.

It was very satisfying to know that we were able to apprehend these burglars before they could do any further damage, steal valuables or physically harm the elderly homeowner. These two chuckleheads should have chosen a different career path. If this had happened in the good ole USA, grandma might have armed herself with a gun and shot through the bedroom door. These young lads were lucky that this is Canada and not the States. On the other hand, this could also have ended in tragedy if these punks had gone into grandma's bedroom. Who knows what could have happened to her if a physical altercation had ensued. It's something I try not to think about.

Break-ins are a violation of one of our most sacred and personal spaces: our homes. Most burglars do not want to get caught and will flee, and nighttime burglaries on residences are also rare. A criminal breaking into an empty home is a concern, but the threat of a home invasion when the residents are at home is what keeps many people awake at night. While most homeowners fear an overnight break-in, crime statistics show that most home break-ins occur during the day, so homeowners are more likely to be surprised by a burglar in the daylight hours than upon awakening from a sound sleep. The elderly woman in my story should have bought a lottery ticket.

Some words of advice before moving on to the next chapter. Keep your windows covered and your garage locked so valuable items are out of sight. Install motion sensor lights, deadbolt locks and upgrade patio/sliding glass door locks. Trim shrubs and bushes to eliminate hiding spots, and never hide keys outside. Don't announce your vacation or trips on social media. Locking your doors and windows is the first and easiest defence against home intruders, but how many of us are doing it consistently? Burglars are often looking for easy targets, and an unlocked door or window is just that. Even when you're home, it's good practice to keep them locked. And when you're leaving the house, double-check doors and first-floor windows to make sure they're all secured.

Unlike the previous story, most burglars don't want to enter your house when you're there. They prefer to break in when no one is home. They also want to be in and out as quickly as possible. Therefore, one of the best ways to prevent intruders is to make it look like someone is home at all times. Installing a home security system is one of the most effective ways to prevent intruders from entering and to alert you if there's been a break-in. Data shows that a home without a security system is roughly three times more likely to be broken into. If an intruder spots a security camera or a sign indicating you have a security system, they'll likely keep moving.

CHAPTER FOUR

Before You Go See The Priest, Leave Your Gun At Home

I believe that this incident may have happened sometime around 1989 or 1990. During one particular evening, I was working as a uniformed patrol officer and was dispatched to a suspicious person call in the area of St. Pius church located on Waverly St. Someone reported seeing a male person walking around and carrying what appeared to be a rifle. It was dark out and the witness couldn't tell for sure if it was an actual firearm or something else.

When you respond to these types of calls, you have to assume that you are dealing with a real gun and you have to prepare for the worst case scenario. The caller was also able to provide a licence plate number of a vehicle that the suspect was seen getting into. I arrived on scene but was not able to locate the suspicious person or the vehicle. Both were GOA (Gone On Arrival). I spoke to the complainant and was able to get a description of the person and vehicle. Then I checked the plate number on our CPIC (Canadian Police Information Centre) system and it came back registered to a male person named McGrinder. He was approximately 35 – 40 years old. I was able to get a phone number and contacted him.

When he answered the phone, I identified myself as a police officer and made him aware of my investigation. At first, he denied being in that area. After more questioning, he admitted that he had gone to the church because he wanted to speak with the priest. However, he denied being in possession of a firearm. He was quite belligerent and uncooperative during our conversation. I told McGrinder to come down to the police station to speak with me but he refused.

He also told me that he had been a police officer up in Sudbury, Ontario during the late 1970's and early 1980's. He said that he had witnessed one of his colleagues being shot to death and later resigned from the police force due to some mental health issues. I asked him if he owned any guns and he confirmed that he did. He wouldn't tell me how many or what type of guns he owned. Then he simply hung up and ended our conversation.

There was something about this that just didn't feel right. I also contacted the Sudbury Police Force and spoke to a Staff Sergeant who confirmed that McGrinder had been a member of their police force and an avid scuba diver. He was also one of their first police officers hired with a university degree. This was the 1970's and much has changed since then. He ended up resigning for personal reasons. The Staff Sergeant did not provide any further details but he did describe McGrinder as a bit of an odd character.

Based on all information received during my initial investigation, I determined that we needed to search the suspect's home and seize his firearms. I felt that any firearms should be removed from the residence while we continued to investigate the circumstances involving the suspicious person incident near the church. The sooner the better. I spoke to my supervisor in regards to this matter. He recommended that I contact the suspect's wife and get her consent to enter and search the residence for the weapons. I made arrangements to go to the house at a time when the suspect wouldn't be there.

I attended the McGrinder residence with a back up officer and spoke to the wife. She confirmed that her husband wasn't home and she agreed to sign a form allowing us to search with her consent. As a result, we didn't have to apply for a search warrant since she had given us permission to enter the dwelling, search and seize the firearms. She even showed us where most of the guns were. We found that the firearms were improperly stored and some of them were even loaded. We also searched for any firearms that may have been hidden. I found a loaded handgun in a dresser drawer located in the bedroom. At the time, the suspect and his wife had a 4-year-old daughter who could have easily gone into the bedroom, opened the dresser drawer and picked up the gun. This could have ended in a terrible tragedy.

The wife thanked us for coming over and taking the guns out of the house. She was emotional and seemed depressed. I asked her if her husband was being abusive towards her or their daughter and she replied that he was not. She admitted that they were having some difficulties in their marriage and that her spouse was struggling with a mental illness.

We transported the firearms to the police station and tagged each one as seized property. This included rifles, shotguns, handguns and ammunition. All of these weapons were legally owned by McGrinder. I submitted a detailed report regarding the suspicious person incident and firearms seizure. The report was forwarded to the Criminal Investigation Section for further follow-up. As a result of the follow-up investigation, McGrinder was charged with careless storage of firearms.

He answered the knock at the door and wanted to know why a police detective had come to his home. He definitely wasn't happy to see Detective Graham standing there. The detective explained the criminal charge and informed the accused that he was being issued a summons to appear in court. The accused refused to accept the summons and Graham placed the summons against McGrinder's chest and said, *"Now, you are served."* The detective turned around and walked away.

McGrinder ended up filing a complaint against Detective Graham, myself and the other uniformed officer who had assisted me with the firearms seizure. In fact, he tried to lay private criminal charges against us. He wanted to charge me and the other officer with theft for stealing his guns. He basically said that we had no right to take away his guns and that they were seized illegally. He also applied to have Detective Graham charged with assault for hitting him in the chest with the summons. He claimed that the detective had slapped the summons against his chest causing him to almost fall backwards.

The way this works is that a justice of the peace will review the complainant's application and decide to either not take action if the allegations do not meet the requirements of the Criminal Code or instruct court staff to prepare an information based on the application. In this case, the justice of the peace concluded that there was not enough evidence or information to substantiate any criminal charges against us.

I've got to be honest and say that I was a little concerned about this guy. He was mentally unstable, had access to guns and had prior training as a police officer. Now it seemed as though he hated cops and was very upset about having his guns taken away from him. I had an uneasy feeling about him and didn't really know what he might be capable of doing. For awhile after this incident occurred, I became more aware of my surroundings. Maybe I was being a little paranoid but I started to worry or think about the possibility that this guy could become unhinged and might try to exact some revenge.

Detective Graham called me at the police station one day. He told me that he had received a strange phone call at his home. He was off duty and when he answered his phone, the unknown caller simply stated, *"You're not that hard to find."* That was all he said and quickly hung up. There was no call display but we figured it was McGrinder who phoned the detective. We couldn't prove it but we were pretty sure it was him. This reaffirmed that my feelings about this guy were valid and real.

There are strict rules regarding the storage of firearms and ammunition in Canada. These are set out under federal law.

The regulations provide very specific instructions for those who have firearms on their property. Ultimately, if you are the person responsible for a firearm, then you must take reasonable precautions to keep others safe. If you fail to do this, then you could be charged with the careless storage of firearms. The improper or careless storage of firearms means that you have put a gun, or ammunition, in an unsafe place. I'm sure that the accused ended up appearing in court for the firearms charge but I don't recall what the outcome was. I'm assuming that he plead guilty since I never received a trial notification. I don't even know if he ever got his guns back. I just hope that he was able to get some help for his mental health issues and that everything turned out well for him and his family.

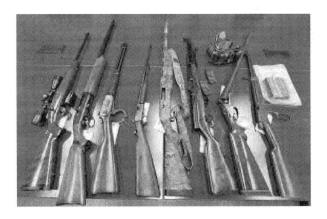

CHAPTER FIVE

Death Stinks

Death stinks, both figuratively and literally. Once you've smelled it, you'll never forget it. The exposure to these unpleasant odours come from attending sudden death investigations and post-mortem examinations, also known as autopsies. I hated going to these types of calls. When you arrive to investigate these incidents, you always hope for a fresh body. The fresh stage, refers to the body right after death, when few signs of decomposition are visible. This could be a suicide, accidental or natural death that occurred very recently. What you don't want is a dead body that's been sitting there for days or even weeks. Of course, we don't get to choose and even the fresh bodies can get pretty messy after a traumatic death. Especially when they involve a suicide by firearm.

After someone has passed away, family and friends get to see the deceased person in a more formal and usually much calmer setting, such as when they are laid out in a funeral home. They look relaxed, calm and often look like they are sleeping. The body has been washed from head to toe and embalmed. Hair shampooed and conditioned. Nails cut, filed, cleaned. Ear and nose hairs trimmed. Eyebrows plucked. Makeup and hair styling included. Hell, I've seen some of the dearly departed who looked much better after death than they did when they were still alive. It's amazing what a professional makeup artist and stylist can do. The deceased is usually an older person such as an elderly parent or grandparent. Sometimes, it's someone much younger. These are the dead bodies that the majority of people will see during their lifetime.

For some reason, there are some people who are terrified or uncomfortable being around a deceased person laid out in a casket. You'll see them at the funeral visitation, hanging out at the back of the room and as far away from the casket as possible. Fortunately, the vast majority of ordinary people will never see the corpse of someone who has just been violently killed, committed suicide or died in a tragic accident. First responders such as police officers, firefighters and paramedics don't have a choice and must attend sudden death incidents when they happen and then have to see all the blood, guts and gore. People might say, *"that's their job."* I say it doesn't make it any easier.

I got dispatched to an apartment building and met with the superintendent. He hadn't seen one of his tenants around for awhile and got a bit worried. This particular tenant hadn't been answering the phone or the door. He let me in and as soon as I entered the apartment unit, I was immediately hit with an unpleasant odour. I knew right away that something was wrong. A second officer arrived on scene. I asked the superintendent to remain in the hallway while we checked out the inside of the apartment. As we walked in, I could see a body lying on the hallway floor just outside of the bedroom. The deceased male had fallen face down onto the hardwood floor. I could also see some dried up blood stains on the floor near his head. All he had on was a shirt.

I did notice quite a few empty and partially consumed bottles of wine and liquor in the kitchen and living room. This guy appeared to be a heavy drinker. Through investigation, we were able to determine that the dead guy was in his fifties and had been previously diagnosed with heart failure. I would have guessed liver failure. He was deemed to have died of natural causes. No murder mystery here. The sad thing is that he was estranged from his family and died alone. The body removal service team arrived and were getting ready to put the deceased in a body bag. As soon as they lifted his head from the floor, the foul odour got worse. It smelled like rotting meat and it looked as though his face had started to melt into the hardwood floor.

The skin had started to separate from the flesh. Underneath him was all mushy. The dead guy's face appeared to be flattened and distorted. This poor guy had obviously been on the floor for a considerable amount of time. I could see some bodily fluids on the ground when they lifted his head. There were maggots crawling around.

This sudden death incident happened on a Saturday day shift. I believe it was during the summer because my wife and I were expecting a few friends over for some barbecue. Well as luck would have it, I ended up having to cook up some hamburgers and hot dogs on the grill. While cooking up the meat, all I could think of was the smell from the dead body. The smell of rotting meat. Needless to say, I wasn't able to eat any of the meat that evening. I just told everyone that I wasn't hungry and had some fruit, snacks and beer instead. I didn't say anything about the dead guy because I didn't want to ruin anyone else's dinner.

This next stinker story also happened inside of an apartment unit but this time, the deceased was female. As I walked up the stairs, I could already smell the body. To make matters worse, it was an extremely hot and humid day. When we found her, she was lying on the bathroom floor with her head stuck to the top ledge of the bath tub. It looked as if she had fallen and hit her head on the side of the tub. It was obvious that rigor mortis had set in. The dead body was going through the stages of decomposition. It looked like she had been there for several days and had maggots all over her. When the body removal service finally got there, it took four of us to pick her up and put her in the body bag. She was a heavy set woman. One of the guys from the removal service lit up a cigar to cover up the smell. We opened up the windows but it didn't help all that much. It was just too damn hot and humid. The second officer who came to back me up was a young rookie. As soon as he entered the apartment unit, he started gagging and coughing. I thought he was going to pass out or throw up but lucky for him, he didn't do either. There were a lot of flies buzzing around as well.

A post-mortem examination determined that this poor woman died of natural causes while sitting on the toilet. She had dropped dead from a massive stroke. It was also determined that she had bleeding in the brain caused by hitting her head on the bathtub when she fell off the toilet seat. She was in her late sixties. We put on our latex gloves and covered the body with a large blanket. We started to pick her up, from the floor, to put her in the body bag. The stench was unbearable, particularly when she was moved and her bodily fluids released. I noticed that some maggots were stuck to my pants. The decaying corpse also released feces from the rectum. As a result of gas build up, the sphincter opened up and some leftover poop was excreted via the anus. You should have seen the rookie's face. I think this was his first dead body call but I was sure it wouldn't be his last.

It's hard to imagine a worse place to die than sitting on the toilet, doing your business. A Chicago police officer once stated, *"I have since learned that this is the way a lot of people go to the great beyond — on the toilet. It's like it's a launching pad to the cosmos or something."*

Strange as it may sound, there's a pretty well established link between dropping a deuce and dropping dead. Most strokes which occur during defecation are a result of the unnatural sitting posture for waste elimination. If one applies excessive strain during defecation, it affects the cardiovascular system, which might result in death. It can also lead to temporary loss of consciousness due to insufficient blood flow to the heart and brain. But people with heart disease or blood pressure disorders, or who take medication for hypertension, are more at risk. For those of you that are more at risk, you may want to avoid excessive straining on the toilet bowl. That includes me!

A good option is to use Metamucil. It works by increasing the bulk of your stool, an effect that helps to cause bowel movements. It also increases the levels of water in the stool, making the stool softer and easier to pass. It could even save your life.

I've also attended some autopsies during my policing career. The most unpleasant part of this is the smell that permeates the air once the inside of the body is exposed during a post-mortem. The smell can also get into your clothing because odour permeates items made of all fabric and other porous material. Sometimes, putting a little bit of Vicks VapoRub under the nostrils will help to cut down on any foul odour. Sometimes it works and sometimes it doesn't.

The body of the deceased is brought into the post-mortem examination room on a stainless steel gurney. Before any incisions are made, the pathologist makes a physical inspection of the body. This includes taking notes of physical characteristics like age, race, and any unusual tattoos or scars. The pathologist uses a scalpel to make a long and deep incision down the front of the body. After completing the incision, the pathologist spreads open the skin and begins to split the rib cage. An electric saw or bone cutter is used to open the rib cage. The internal organs from the chest cavity are removed and examined.

A mini electric saw is then used to make a cut from ear to ear on the lower back of the head. After the incision, the scalp is cut and separated from the underlying skull and pulled forward. The bone saw is then used to cut open the top of the skull so that the brain can also be removed and examined for any signs of aneurysm, stroke or other potential causes of death. The smell of burnt bone is purely rancid but the real bad smell usually comes along after the colon or intestines are exposed, nicked or cut. The pathologist will slice the internal organs into sections looking for injury or disease. The body is opened in a manner that does not interfere with an open casket service.

I hated going to these post-mortems but like I've said before, you don't get to choose. It's bad enough no matter what age the deceased person is but it's a lot worse if it's the corpse of a young person. An autopsy is a detailed dissection of a deceased person, done to determine why they died. When a person dies – especially if it's unexpectedly or violently – their loved ones want answers. Many questions accompany these types of deaths. The autopsy is an important key to finding these answers. Post-mortems can also be an important way for families and loved ones to seek reassurance or peace of mind after a death. The thorough examination of the deceased may help to reduce the stress of the unknown for the family members.

"Nope. Looks to me like a clear-cut case of suicide by somehow reaching around behind the back and sticking a knife in backward. Let's get a drink."

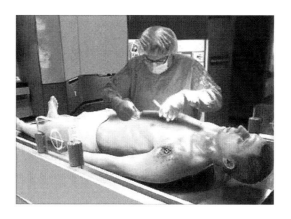

CHAPTER SIX

The Carnival Comes To Town

You can smell the funnel cakes, the petting zoo, the cotton candy and see the bright lights. You can hear the whizzing, whirling sounds of the rides. There are few things that say "carnival" more than the scent of freshly spun cotton candy and funnel cake bubbling in the deep fryer. Kids and adults alike get all excited when a carnival comes to town. The food, games and the rides. It's all about some good old fashioned fun!

Oh, and did I mention the local yokels and riff-raff that tend to gravitate towards these types of events? Thieves and drug dealers also come out to play at the "carnival." It's the responsibility of the police to keep an eye out for these miscreants.

The people who organize these special events will often hire off-duty officers to provide police presence. These are what we call Paid Duty or Special Duty Officers. They provide security, crowd and traffic control. These officers are paid by the organizers of the events and not by the taxpayers. Twenty-three year-old Police Officer Brian was the Special Duty cop assigned to patrol the Civic Centre where the travelling carnival was being held. It was a Friday evening in April. As he walked through the carnival site, he noticed a few familiar faces in the crowd. Also milling about the carnival were the local troublemakers. One of his duties would be to keep an eye on these guys. Who knows what they were up to.

This was not an undercover operation. Brian was in full uniform and he wanted these guys to know that he was there. Several times he would make eye contact with them and even acknowledge them by name. He also made it a point to stop and talk to them. Just a little bit of small talk like, *"Hey Robby, how's it going? Have you been staying out of trouble lately? Aren't you on probation right now?"* You know, that type of conversation.

A little later into the evening, Brian noticed a couple of guys that seemed to be acting a little suspicious. As the officer approached them, they started walking away in different directions. Well, at least they knew that the police were there and that they had better be on their best behaviour. A few minutes later, Brian could hear loud banging noises and people yelling nearby. There was some kind of a noisy disturbance going on. He ran towards the commotion and as he got closer, he could see a young man damaging the aluminum wall siding of some carnival concession booths. He had gone berserk and was trying to rip this one booth apart with his bare hands.

Officer Brian ordered the lunatic to stop damaging the property but he just looked directly at the officer and told him to *"Fuck off."* Brian moved in closer and grabbed him by the right arm to restrain him. A struggle ensued and both ended up falling to the ground. The officer was attempting to make an arrest when all of a sudden, he was assaulted and kicked in the head by two other young men. They repeatedly kicked him while he was on the ground trying to handcuff the suspect who was actively resisting. It was a disgusting and cowardly attack perpetrated against this young officer. He was just doing his job and trying to keep the community safe.

Brian was taken to the hospital after it became apparent that he was confused. He was suffering from a concussion, partial amnesia, a chipped tooth and injuries to his cheek and eye. Due to his head injury and possible severe concussion, the officer was kept in hospital overnight for observation and was listed in fair condition.

During the incident, carnival workers assisted the officer as he was being assaulted and were able to hold on to two suspects until other officers arrived on scene to make the arrest. Hooray for the carnies! As a result, police arrested and charged a 17-year-old youth and a 19-year-old male. Both were charged with assault causing bodily harm and assaulting a police officer. One other 19-year-old male was charged with mischief (vandalism) over one thousand dollars.

All three accused persons appeared in court for a bail hearing. I don't know if there was ever a trial for these punks or what kind of punishment they received for their violent behaviour towards the police officer. But I do know that it was another fun night at the carnival!

"Hurry, hurry, step right up!"

CHAPTER SEVEN

Hit and Run

On a hit-and-run in baseball, the base runner will only start running once they know that the pitcher is committed to delivering a pitch. The runner gets a head start and begins to run to the next base as the pitcher delivers the ball to the batter, who must try to hit it in order to protect the runner. The batter in a hit-and-run scenario must swing at the pitch. Hopefully, the hitter can put the ball in play, and the runner will be able to advance the bases. It's just a game and usually, no one gets seriously injured or killed.

Then there is another kind of hit and run that involves vehicles and sometimes pedestrians. Failure to remain at the scene of an accident under the Highway Traffic Act is a traffic ticket, a violation of the driving laws of Ontario and is considered a breach of a provincial statute under the Ontario Highway Traffic Act. Failure to stop at the scene of an accident is a federal criminal code offence, under the Criminal Code of Canada and is considered a criminal offence. Being charged with either offence is a serious matter which can affect your right to drive, livelihood and you could even face jail time. Most of the time, these types of hit and run involve property damage only. Sometimes they involve serious injuries and even death.

It was summertime Saturday and I was assigned to the uniform patrol section. I was working the night shift and it had been a hot and humid evening. The booze had surely been flowing at the local liquor establishments. There would have been lots of house parties along with a few bush parties. We were getting hit with all kinds of calls involving noise complaints, disorderly drunks, fights, disturbances, impaired drivers and domestic disputes.

It was just after 2:00 a.m. and the temperature had cooled off somewhat. I was dispatched to a report of a pedestrian hit by a car on West Street, not far from the downtown area. Paramedics were also notified to respond. I wasn't too far from the scene and got there before the ambulance crew. As I approached the accident scene, I could see something on the roadway. As I got closer, I could tell that it was a person lying on the ground. I immediately stopped and blocked the lane with the police cruiser to prevent other drivers from running over the male person that was on the road. I made sure the flashing, emergency roof lights were on before I exited my vehicle. I noticed that a crowd of onlookers had started to gather to see what was going on. As I approached, I told everyone to step back.

The injured person was lying on his side and moaning. I bent over and saw that he was conscious and breathing. He looked to be in his late teens or early twenties. There was blood on his face and he had injuries in the lower part of his body. I could see part of a bone protruding from just below his right knee. His leg appeared swollen and bruised. Surprisingly, the young man didn't seem to be in much pain. With the kind injuries that I observed, I would have thought that he would be crying out in pain. I was worried that he was going to go into shock and lose consciousness.

I grabbed an emergency blanket from the trunk of the cruiser and placed it on the victim. I noticed he had some cuts and abrasions to the lips and jaw. He also had numerous scrapes and bruises on his arms and legs. His shirt was ripped at the shoulder and had blood on it. I was also concerned about possible internal bleeding. As I knelt down beside him, he looked at me and asked if he was going to be okay. He appeared to be trembling and said that he didn't want to die. I held his hand and could see the fear in his eyes. I kept telling him to stay awake, reassuring him that the ambulance was on its way and that he would be alright. I could hear the distant wail of a siren and felt relieved knowing that the paramedics would soon be arriving.

Other officers were now on scene and directing traffic. The ambulance arrived shortly and began looking after the injured pedestrian. After he struck the pedestrian, the driver of the car took off without stopping to render any assistance to the injured man. I spoke to some witnesses that had observed the accident and they were able to provide me with a description of the vehicle and a partial licence plate number. One of the witnesses told me that there were two people in the vehicle.

I took written statements from the witnesses and began filling out a motor vehicle accident report and a hit and run collision report. The victim was transported to hospital. There are several reasons why some drivers will flee an accident scene. They may not have a valid driver's licence or insurance, they could be impaired by drugs or alcohol, they could be in a stolen vehicle or might have a prior record with outstanding warrants for arrest.

I later attended the hospital to get some additional information on the victim's identity and his injuries. The twenty-one-year-old male suffered a broken leg, a separated shoulder, a concussion and had several teeth knocked out. Once the reports were completed, I forwarded them to the Traffic Section for review. An investigator was assigned to do the follow-up on the hit and run. As a result of the investigation, a 27-year-old male was arrested and charged with failing to remain at the scene of an accident and criminal negligence causing bodily harm.

The investigation also revealed that as the driver fled the accident scene, he ignored the passenger's plea to return after he saw the young man lying on the road. He eventually plead guilty and was sentenced to ninety days in jail for leaving the scene of an accident. The judge also agreed that a jail term was necessary as a deterrent to others. The sad thing is that the victim of this hit and run could have been left lying on the road for some time before receiving any help. He could also have been run over by other vehicles. The good news is that he survived his injuries and hopefully was able to make a full recovery.

If you are a pedestrian, follow the rules of the road and obey signs and signals. Walk on sidewalks whenever they are available. If there is no sidewalk, walk facing traffic and as far from traffic as possible. Cross streets at crosswalks or intersections. Look for cars in all directions, including those turning left or right. If you have been consuming alcoholic beverages, you should take a taxi or an Uber to get home safely. Yes, walking while drunk can also be dangerous to your health.

If you are the driver of a motor vehicle, make sure you follow the rules of the road and obey signs and signals. If you have been consuming alcoholic beverages, then have someone else drive that hasn't been consuming such beverages. Or you can take a taxi, an Uber or have someone pick you up and drive you home.

If you do happen to hit another vehicle or a pedestrian, please STOP! For God's sake, STOP! and provide assistance. Call 9-1-1 immediately and stay put. If you leave the scene of an accident, you will get caught! You might end up having to do some jail time. Especially if someone is injured or killed as a result of your careless or dangerous driving.

CHAPTER EIGHT

The Mundane Parts Of The Job

Police work isn't always as exciting or as glamorous as you might see on TV or in the movies. If you are watching police officers on the screen, you would think that this job constantly has you on the edge of your seat. You would think that there was so much excitement going on every minute of every shift. After all, look at all the high-speed car chases and police shootouts on the screen. Police work is interesting and challenging, but it's not a thrill a minute. While real-life officers have their share of heart-pounding moments, it's the less glorified tasks that tend to take up the majority of an officer's shift.

The thrill of the chase

On TV, all crimes are solved within an hour or two. The life of a TV cop is loaded with drama. Car chases, bar fights, undercover stings, drug raids, kicking in doors and shooting the bad guys. All done without ever having to fill out an incident or arrest report. All the excitement without the paperwork. What a dream! It's just a whirlwind of excitement. People actually apply to become police officers based on what they have seen on TV. They think that police work is so cool and exciting that they actually want to become cops so that they can experience this kind of life.

Now don't get me wrong. Do police shootings happen in real life? Of course they do. Do cops get involved in car chases and foot pursuits? Of course they do. But not as often as Hollywood would want you to believe. Have you ever watched the TV series called COPS? For those of you who have never heard of this program, it's a reality show about real police officers responding to actual calls for service. Television camera crews accompany the officers as they perform their duties. I remember reading somewhere that the camera crew had to ride along with the cops and video tape scenes for a couple of weeks before they were able to get enough material to produce a 30-minute episode.

Camera crew follows police officers on the job

Samples of boring types of calls that I have responded to:

- A local variety store employee calls to complain about someone harassing customers in the parking lot. The homeless guy is there when I arrive. I tell him to leave the property and he does.

- A call about kids throwing rocks at passing vehicles. When I arrive, they are gone (GOA). Apparently no vehicles were struck as no victims came forward to complain of damage.

- A residential panic alarm turns out to be false. This involved an elderly woman wearing a Medical Alert alarm pendant that can be worn as a necklace. These can truly be lifesavers. The elderly lady apologized profusely when she realized that she had accidentally pressed the alarm button. She seemed embarrassed but I told her not to worry and that we were just glad she was okay. She promised she would be more careful.

- Directing traffic at a major intersection. Lights are out and I have to standby and keep the traffic moving safely while city crews are working to repair the lights.

Police officer directing traffic at an intersection

- Dispatched to a parking complaint. When I get there, the vehicle is gone. It was moved prior to my arrival.

- Dispatched to a residential alarm call. The exterior of the home appears to be secure. No broken windows or doors. We wait for the key holder to respond so that we can enter the house and check the inside. About thirty minutes later, the homeowner arrives to let us in.

We enter the residence and find that everything appears to be in order. Possible alarm malfunction. We obtain the name and date of birth of the owner/key holder and clear the call as a false alarm with no report. The vast majority of burglar alarm calls (94-99 percent) turn out to be false. What a waste of time.

Sorry officer. I accidentally set off the alarm. Everything's okay.

- Domestic dispute call comes in. Myself along with a backup officer respond. Boyfriend and girlfriend arguing about some missing money. It apparently got really loud and some neighbours called the police. The boyfriend left before we arrived on scene and the woman didn't want to to discuss it any further with us. We cleared the call with no report.

- Another domestic dispute call comes in for us to attend an apartment where a male and female are supposedly fighting. This was also called in by neighbours who heard, yelling, screaming and things being thrown around. We get there and are told by both the male and female that we are not needed. No assault has taken place and everything appears to be in order. We clear the scene and go to our next call.

- I respond to a 9-1-1 hang-up call. On arrival, we find an elderly couple sitting on the front porch of the residence. Everything looks normal. I am told that there is no problem here and that everything is okay. I don't see anything to suggest otherwise so I clear the call.

- I'm in court most of the morning waiting to testify for a criminal case. The accused pleads guilty to one charge of assault while a second charge is withdrawn. A trial is avoided and I don't have to testify. I go back on patrol.

Police officers waiting to testify in court

- I am dispatched to a motor vehicle accident. The weather is snowy and wet. Several car accidents have been reported as a result of the slippery roads. The accident that I go to is a simple one with minor damage and no injuries. One vehicle slid into another due to inclement weather.

Minor motor vehicle accident on icy road

- A vehicle has stalled in traffic. The owner has already called for a tow truck. I stand by until the tow truck arrives so that the broken down vehicle doesn't get hit by another vehicle. I activate the roof lights and block the lane with my cruiser. Once the vehicle is towed, I clear the call and resume patrol.

- I get dispatched to a convenience store parking lot in the north end of the city. Someone called to say that two guys are sitting in a vehicle selling drugs and smoking marijuana. We get there and don't see anyone in the parking lot. We check the area but are unable to locate the vehicle or any suspicious activities. We clear the call and move on to the next one.

- Escort a funeral procession going from the church to the cemetery. When I arrive at the front entrance of our destination, I exit the police cruiser and stand at attention to salute the hearse as it passes by along with the limousine transporting the grieving family. I then clear the call and resume patrol.

Escorts are also provided for processions going from the funeral home to the church. In Ontario, funeral processions without police escort must follow all the usual rules of the road. If a procession vehicle goes through a red light and a crash results, Highway Traffic Act charges will apply.

Police cruiser leading a funeral procession

- I respond to a barking dog complaint. An anonymous person has called to report that the dog in the neighbourhood is continuously barking and disrupting his life. He is sick and tired of this and wants police to do something about it. I speak with the dog owner and advise him of the complaint. I also make him aware of the city noise bylaw. He apologizes and tells me that he will try and keep the dog as quiet as possible. Yeah, good luck with that.

A constantly barking dog can be loud and can disturb you or your neighbours. Back in the day, we use to respond to numerous calls for barking dog complaints every year. It was a frustrating type of call to respond to. I believe that we now have bylaw enforcement officers who deal with these types of complaints instead of police officers.

- My next call is a Landlord and Tenant Dispute. After listening to both parties whining and complaining, I tell them that this is a civil matter and not a police matter. Neither person is happy with my response as each expected that the police take their side. I tell them to keep the peace and to file an application for a hearing. I clear the call, hoping that I don't have to return.

- Another alarm goes off at an office building in the north end of the city. I'm responding from the west end of the city. Somehow, I still get there before my backup officer arrives. When I get there, I can see a cleaning crew inside the building. Apparently, they entered the building and accidentally set off the alarm system. Another waste of time.

- I get dispatched to a noise complaint. Someone is playing loud music and disturbing the neighbours. I arrive on scene and speak with the homeowner. He says he always plays his music loud and no one has ever complained before. So, now he wants to know what the problem is. I tell him that some neighbours have complained about the loud music and I also explained the noise bylaw to him.

  I told him to turn the music down. He complies with my request and I move on to my next call. Each time that I go to these types of calls, I also have to obtain the name of the person and their date of birth. The information then gets entered into the computer system. This way, we can keep track of how many times we end up going to the same address for noise complaints.

- I was walking the beat in the downtown area and checking for parking violations. This was during the day shift (8:00 a.m. to 6:00 p.m.) I spent the next couple of hours chalking tires and then returning later to issue tickets to vehicles for overtime parking violations. My boss at the time really loved it when his officers brought in lots of parking tickets. I guess parking violations were his pet peeve. I indulged him and remained in his good books. After all, I was just a rookie and following orders. Thankfully, these types of parking violations are now handled by municipal bylaw enforcement officers and not the police.

Police officer issues parking ticket

- Working the day shift (7:00 a.m. to 5:00 p.m.) and set up radar speed enforcement on one of the busy streets in town. Radar equipment was tested and found to be working properly. Pointed radar gun towards oncoming traffic and waited for the next speeder. Pulled over numerous vehicles and issued a quantity of tickets and some warnings. A radar gun is the kind of gun that saves lives instead of taking lives. It causes drivers to slow down. It's the kind of gun I prefer to use on the job.

Police officer operating a radar gun

It feels exciting doesn't it? Just like on TV and the movies. Should I keep listing more of the boring duties or do you get the idea? I could go on and on. I could fill an entire book with all the tedious and monotonous calls that police officers have to deal with on a daily basis. I could but I won't. I think some of you readers might be craving more. Okay then, I'll give you a bunch more of these and then I'll move on. You asked for it.

- I got dispatched to a silent hold-up alarm coming from a downtown bank. I had to respond from the east end of the city. An officer was already on scene waiting for my arrival. We cautiously entered the bank in case this was the real thing. We spoke with the bank manager who told us that the alarm was accidentally activated by one of the employees. He apologized for wasting our time. I put the information in my notebook and cleared the call.

- I respond to 9-1-1 calls coming from a home in the south end of the city. A woman answers the door looking very surprised that police are there. I tell her about the 9-1-1 calls that we had received from her residence. She tells me everything is just fine. I can hear children talking and laughing in the background. I find out that the kids were playing with the phone and decided to give 9-1-1 a try. It was time for an Officer Rick lecture about the proper use of 9-1-1 and mom gave her kids a real tongue lashing.

> To the police department,
>
> I am very sorry that I called you when there wasn't ony emergency. We kept saying the wrong odress to trick you. We did it because we thought it was funny. Please forgive me. I will do anything to get out of jail if you send me there. I promise not to do it again. I want to stay home. I would never do that again

Written apology letter to the police from one of the boys who took part in the prank 9-1-1 calls

- The next call is for some teenagers shooting off fireworks in a school playground with younger kids around. I arrive on scene and there's nobody in the playground and no sign of any fireworks being set off. I clear the call and resume patrol.

- We responded to a report of loiterers at a shopping plaza. Prior to our arrival, the loiterers left the area.

- Caller advised of a male screaming at the bus stop. We respond to the location and locate a male youth. I spoke with him and he said that he was just fine and was waiting for the bus. There was no problem but he may have been talking a little loud. He was advised to keep it down.

- I responded to a loud music complaint at an apartment building. After I spoke with some of the residents who had complained, I advised the offending resident to keep the volume on his music down.

- Dispatched to a minor accident. A pickup truck was struck by another vehicle, causing minor damage to the passenger rear side of the truck. A minor accident report was competed and the persons involved were given an incident number for insurance purposes. I believe they decided to settle it on their own.

- Responded to a call about some teenagers loitering and causing a ruckus in front of a grocery store. We arrived on scene and observed nine male youths in the parking lot. They were told to leave and not to return.

- We got a call in regards to a suspicious person trying to get into the lobby of an apartment building. We checked the area with negative results. Person was gone on arrival.

- Responded to a Break and Enter in progress. We found a male youth inside the residence who identified himself as the son of the homeowner. He had some identification on him and we called his father at his place of employment to confirm. Apparently, the teenager had lost his keys and decided to enter the house through an unlocked window.

- Dispatched to a 9-1-1 call. Complainant reporting that her grandson was yelling and banging at the front door. She believed that he was high on drugs and trying to get into the house. He was gone when we arrived on scene.

- I respond to a neighbour dispute that has been going on for weeks. One neighbour keeps throwing dog shit into the other neighbour's backyard. No one has actually seen him do it but he's the only one who owns a dog in close proximity. The complainant has also threatened to kick the dog owner's ass if he continues to fling poop over the fence. I warned him about making threats of violence towards his neighbour. I spoke to the dog owner and he denied throwing the poop over the fence and wanted his neighbour arrested for threatening him. I told him that his neighbour had already been warned about making threats.

I also said that if we were to obtain a sample of his dog's poop, we would be able to do a DNA comparison with the poop being thrown over the fence. This was just a ploy to get him to admit it. I had no intention of seizing any samples of shit. He said he would never give me a sample without a warrant. I also advised him that his neighbour was going to be installing a security camera in his backyard. I made it clear that if this crap continued, he would be arrested and charged with Mischief (obstructing, interrupting or interfering with any person in the lawful use and enjoyment of their property). Thankfully, we didn't receive any further calls from these people. Problem solved.

Shit happens

Neighbour dispute

In reality and as opposed to what you see on television, police do fight crime, to be sure — but they are mainly called upon to be social workers and referees that mediate or resolve disputes between family members, landlords and tenants, quarrelsome neighbours, etc. They are also traffic and parking enforcers, accident investigators, mental health counsellors, detailed report writers, sometimes all in the span of a single shift. In fact, the overwhelming majority of officers spend only a small fraction of their time responding to violent crime. This is true of all jurisdictions that include both smaller and larger cities throughout North America. When people choose to go into the field of police work, they think of the action and adventure. They rarely think of the common situations and mundane encounters the police have, like the ones I've mentioned in this chapter.

However, there is no such thing as a routine call. Police officers have been seriously injured or even killed while answering the seemingly routine or boring type of calls. Sometimes police officers get complacent because they respond to so many dead end calls. These include residential and commercial false alarms, suspicious persons or vehicles that are gone on arrival, traffic stops, noise complaints, loitering complaints and many others. As a result, the officers tend to let their guard down. That's why when you respond to any type of call, you need to be ready for the unexpected. You can't be thinking that you're going to a false alarm even before you get there. You have to proceed as if it is the real thing and then be prepared to deal with it when you arrive on scene.

An interesting thing that a police officer told me years ago when I was just a rookie and wet behind the ears. The older officer probably had about fifteen or twenty years of experience under his belt and I listened to him very carefully. He told me that for every call that you respond to as a police officer, there will always be at least one gun present when you arrive at the scene. What does this mean? The next chapter will illustrate the comment made by the old-timer cop.

CHAPTER NINE

There Will Always Be At Least One Gun There When You Arrive At The Scene

On September 14, 1981 one of our police officers was already thinking about the end of his shift. Police Officer Rick (Not me) had started at midnight and would be on his way home by 8:00 a.m. that morning. This was a Monday morning. We're not talking about a Friday or Saturday night. Rick was patrolling his zone at approximately 5:45 a.m. on a Monday morning. Most people were just getting out bed to get ready for work. All of a sudden, a call came in to our dispatch office.

The dispatcher received information that a van had just struck four parked cars in the area of Elgin Street and Stanley Street. The van left the area and officers responded to search for the wanted vehicle. Police Officer Rick was thirty years old and was a six-year veteran with the force. He drove towards the crash scene and on his way there, he observed a van being driven in an erratic manner. He got behind the vehicle and activated his roof lights. He attempted to stop the van but the driver took off and refused to pull over. This was now turning into a high-speed chase.

Rick quickly notified the dispatcher and advised that he was in pursuit of the vehicle wanted for dangerous driving and fail to remain. He radioed his location and direction of travel along with the description of the vehicle. Police Officer Dan heard the emergency broadcast and started making his way over to assist in the vehicle pursuit. They were going to try and block him in, stop the van and arrest the driver. Sounds pretty simple.

During the chase, the van slowed down and the driver jumped out while it was still moving. He took off on foot as the vehicle crashed into a hydro pole. The police cruisers driven by Rick and Dan collided when they tried to avoid hitting the guy after ditching his vehicle on Rawdon Street. The police cars were coming from opposite directions, swerved to miss the suspect and struck each other. Both cruisers were heavily damaged. Looking back now, they should have just run him over and ended it right then and there. However, police officers are trained to serve and protect. Not to run over people.

Both officers exited their police cruisers and chased the suspect on foot. The culprit ran through a number of backyards, ending up at the rear of a house located on Nelson Street. Officers Rick and Dan located him in the backyard of the residence as he was in the process of climbing a fence. They pulled him from the fence and brought him to the ground. The suspect fell on his left side and one of the officers landed on top of him. Both officers attempted to place him under arrest but they were struggling with a combative criminal while yelling at him to stop resisting.

In the ensuing struggle, one of the officers applied a headlock to the suspect while the other tried to gain control of his arms to apply the handcuffs. Unbeknownst to both of them, the violent perpetrator had removed a service revolver from one of the police holsters and was now holding the gun in his right hand. There was a loud BANG! A single shot had been fired and Rick was hit in the upper thigh. The bullet then exited through the back of the thigh and entered the palm of his right hand at the base of the thumb, travelled up the arm and exited just above the elbow.

The suspect then turned the firearm towards Dan. The officer was able to quickly grab his wrist and struggled with him in order to get control of the gun. Dan managed to get on top of the guy and even though he wouldn't release the weapon, Dan was attempting to disarm him by repeatedly punching him in the head while twisting his wrist. A desperate struggle for the weapon ensued. It was literally a life-or-death situation as one officer had already been shot. The suspect dropped the gun and was finally disarmed as more officers arrived on scene. Dan attempted to place handcuffs on him. He was able to cuff one of the arms but could not get both arms close enough together to get the other cuff on. It took the efforts of four officers to get the suspect under control and get the second handcuff on. This goof must have been tripping on angel dust (PCP) or acid (LSD). Rick was lying on the ground suffering from gunshot wounds. He was conscious and breathing.

The gun used in the shooting was a standard issue .38-calibre revolver that was carried by police officers back then. In total, Rick sustained four wounds. Two of them were entrance wounds and the other two were exit wounds. While waiting for the ambulance crew to arrive, an officer grabbed the first aid kit from the trunk of his cruiser. He and another officer applied direct pressure to stop the bleeding by using some sterile gauze pads. The wounded officer was rushed to the Brantford General Hospital where he was listed in fair condition in the intensive care unit. Thankfully, he survived his injuries.

Clearly, the result could have been catastrophically worse. We could have had two officers shot that morning and both could have been killed. The 23-year-old suspect was arrested and charged with attempted murder. Rick sustained serious but non-life-threatening injuries and was expected to make a full recovery. Several years later, he resigned from the police force and opened up his own small business. Good for him!

The criminal who shot Rick had been out all night driving around in a stolen van and breaking into local businesses. I guess you could say that he was working the night shift. When they searched the van, they found break-in tools, an assortment of stolen property along with some marijuana, hash oil and a small amount of heroin. Gee, I wonder why he didn't stop after crashing into those parked vehicles?

You can only imagine the amount of paperwork that would have been generated by this incident. This included painstaking and time-consuming investigations of the hit and run collisions involving a stolen vehicle, commercial break and enters, possession of stolen property and illicit drugs. Let's not forget the attempted murder of a police officer. What a nightmare! As you can see, this story had a high-speed police chase, foot chase through several backyards and over fences and a police officer being shot. Just like in the movies. It just goes to prove that these things can and do happen in real life.

Remember what the old-timer cop told me years ago when I was a rookie? He said, *"There will always be at least one gun there when you arrive at the scene."* The gun he was talking about is the police officer's gun. It's always there no matter where the officer goes. It's quite ironic that the guns carried by cops to protect themselves and other citizens, are the same guns that could potentially be taken from the cops and used against them.

In fact, this is how numerous police officers have been wounded or killed in the line of duty. Just nine days after the Brantford incident, a Toronto cop was shot in the chest and killed with his own gun. The suspect was able to grab the officer's firearm during a physical confrontation. The officer's partner was shot in the hand. The suspect then pointed the gun at two other officers arriving at the scene. One of them fired his weapon and seriously wounded the suspect. Over the years, there have been other incidents but there are just too many to mention or write about.

Some equipment issues came up as a result of these incidents. These were issues being faced by police departments throughout Canada. The first problem was in regards to the police holsters used to carry the firearms. Some of you old-timers might remember the flap holster.

FLAP HOLSTERS:

used by police until the early 1980's

WW1 British Army (1943)

American Civil War (1863)

.38-caliber revolver used by police until the mid-1990's

For obvious reasons, these holsters was commonly referred to as "Widow Makers." All you had to do was pull up the flap and take the revolver out of the holster. Some officers had their guns fall out of these holsters during foot chases. These were extremely unsafe and yet they had been used by Canadian law enforcement officers for more than seventy years.

These ancient holsters were even used by the military during the American Civil War and both World Wars. It was time for a change and thankfully, by the time I was hired by the Brantford Police in 1985, they had already transitioned to a new and modern style holster. These were much safer for the police to use and they may have saved many lives over the years.

The modern holsters have improved greatly over the years. They have built in security features which makes it much more difficult for someone to grab an officer's gun. However, nothing is foolproof and a police officer could potentially be disarmed during a scuffle with a determined and hostile adversary. Fortunately, it doesn't happen as often as it used to.

The second problem pertaining to equipment issues had to do with protective vests or body armour. In the case of Police Officer Rick, a bullet resistant vest would not have made a difference because he was shot in the upper thigh and arm. These are areas of the body that are not protected by body armour. However, it can protect your vital organs if you are shot in the upper body/chest area. The officer in Toronto may have survived the shooting if he had been wearing a vest.

In 1981, regular police officers did not have access to protective vests. For one thing, the vests that did exist were large and cumbersome. They were mainly issued to and used by tactical officers. That would include members of the Emergency Task Force, Emergency Services Unit, Emergency Response

Unit and SWAT (**S**pecial **W**eapons **A**nd **Ta**ctics). These are specialized units called in to deal with hostage situations and barricaded suspects. You get the idea. Back then, they were not made available to regular patrol officers. After several shootings and deaths, things started to change. Unfortunately, people have to get seriously injured or killed before any real changes are made.

When I first became a police officer during the mid 1980's, the members of our force were allowed to decide for themselves whether or not to wear bullet resistant vests. Right after Rick was shot, a police board meeting took place in Brantford the very next day. During the meeting, the police chief stated that *"In light of the Monday morning shooting of one of our officers, more members might want the added protection."* Several years later, wearing the vests became mandatory. Over the years, the quality of soft body armour has significantly improved. It provides greater comfort and protection. As a result, countless lives have been saved.

CHAPTER TEN

Pyjamas And A Deck Of Cards

He kept pacing up and down the sidewalk while his partner in crime kept an eye out for any police officers patrolling in the area. He was bigger than most young persons his age. This guy was about 5'-7" and probably weighed around 150 lbs. He was wearing blue jeans, a black coloured parka with hood up and a navy blue wool scarf around his neck. He kept looking up and down the street as if waiting for something to happen. At about 7:00 p.m., his partner gave the all-clear signal to indicate that he was good to go. He took one more look down the street, wrapped the scarf around the nose and mouth and walked in.

The middle aged variety store clerk was stocking some shelves when the "customer" came in. She heard the door chime and started to walk back to the front counter. It wasn't unusual to see people wearing scarves around their faces. It was early March and extremely cold. Below seasonal temperatures were expected to stick around until at least the end of the week. The clerk tried to make small talk and the recent weather was definitely a conversation starter. She immediately felt shivers down her spine but it wasn't from the cold weather. It was the way he looked at her. He was standing directly in front of her as if he was frozen. He stood there without uttering a sound. His piercing eyes appeared to be staring right through her.

He put his right hand into his coat pocket as he continued staring intensely at the clerk. At this point, she had this awful and foreboding feeling as if something bad was about to happen. Seconds later, the young man pulled out a large knife from the inside of his coat pocket. The woman suddenly let out a shriek and flinched backwards. He slowly moved towards the counter with his right arm extended and holding the knife pointed towards her.

While brandishing the knife, he told the clerk to open the cash register and give him the money inside. He also told her to put packages of cigarettes in a plastic bag. When she refused to comply, he quickly reached over the counter with the knife. He pointed at the cash register and repeated his demands. Although, he didn't do a very good job of disguising himself. While he was yelling at the clerk to give him the money and cigarettes, the scarf fell off and his face was exposed. The employee was stunned when she saw his face and realized for the first time, that he was just a young kid.

The frightened clerk also realized that this guy wasn't playing around and was deadly serious. At one point she thought he was going to jump over the counter and stab her with the knife. That's when she decided to comply with his demands and just give him what he wanted. After she handed over some cash and cigarettes, the suspect ran out of the store and fled on foot. Thankfully, the employee was not physically hurt during the incident but she was visibly shaken. The suspect's trusted lookout was nowhere to be found. He had already taken off and left his partner holding the bag both figuratively and literally.

The clerk immediately called 9-1-1 to report the armed robbery. Uniformed patrol officers responded quickly and began searching the area for the suspect. A description was broadcast to all units along with the direction of travel. Officers also requested an OPP canine unit. This was back in the day when we didn't have our own canine unit and had to rely on the OPP and other jurisdictions. The OPP canine tracked the area of the suspect's departure for a while but eventually lost the scent.

I was doing some followup and paperwork in the Criminal Investigation Section, otherwise known as the detective office. I was notified by the duty Staff Sergeant of an armed robbery that had just occurred at a variety store on Colborne Street. Patrol officers were searching the area for a suspect described as a male youth. At the time, I was assigned to work in the Youth Section where we dealt with incidents involving young persons. We also investigated missing juveniles, otherwise known as runaways. Sometimes we even dealt with kids that were younger than twelve years of age. There wasn't much we could do with kids that young other than giving them a big lecture and notifying the Children's Aid Society (CAS).

Back then, we had the Young Offenders Act (YOA) which was a federal legislation that dealt with young people who were involved in criminal activity. This applied to youths from twelve to seventeen years old. A suspect had to be at least twelve years of age before they could be charged with a criminal offence. The YOA was frequently denounced by opponents as being too lenient on young persons convicted of criminal offences. Some thought that the YOA should have been called the Young, Misdirected and Misguided Children Act (YMMCA). The YOA was eventually replaced by the Youth Criminal Justice Act (YCJA) on April 1, 2003. April Fools Day. How appropriate. Perhaps they were trying to tell us something. The YCJA wasn't all that much better according to the same opponents of the YOA.

I left the detective office and was on my way to the variety store. I radioed the dispatcher and told her to put me on the armed robbery call. Information was received that the suspect may have touched both the counter and cash register when he reached over. This was significant because he wasn't wearing any gloves and may have left some fingerprints behind. As a result, a Scenes Of Crime Officer (SOCO) attended as well.

When I arrived, I met with the store clerk and interviewed her. There had been no other witnesses to the robbery. At the time, the information that we had was that there was only one suspect involved. I also inquired about the store security camera and was able to review the surveillance video. It was very disappointing. This was back in 1998 and the video quality was terrible. The footage appeared to be grainy or blurry and of low-quality. Nevertheless, the surveillance video was seized as part of the investigation.

A week later, our Crime Stoppers tip line received confidential information from a tipster. The information was processed and forwarded to me for follow-up investigation. The anonymous caller provided the name of a possible suspect involved in the variety store hold-up. I ran the name through the CPIC computer system and got a hit. This means that the suspect's name was on file because of previous charges. This criminal was only thirteen years old. He had never done any jail time but had previously been charged with theft related to shoplifting and possession of stolen property. I checked the records office and was able to obtain a photo of the suspect that we had on file. I put together a group of photographs (including the suspect's photo) so that I could conduct a photo lineup. This is a procedure in which an array of photographs is displayed to a victim or a witness to determine if the they can recognize or identify a person involved with the crime. I set up an appointment to have the store clerk attend the station and view the photo lineup.

The police service has a written policy and procedure that dictates how a photo lineup is to be conducted. I will spare you the lengthy and boring details. While viewing the photos, she pointed to the photograph of the suspect and said, *"I'm sure that's him. He's the kid that was in the store with the knife. I'll never forget his face."* Although this was very good information, I still needed more evidence. I had enough to at least bring him in for questioning.

Myself and a uniformed patrol officer attended at the suspect's last known address. The mother answered the door. She was very cooperative and agreed to come down to the station with her son for a videotaped interview. We drove both the mother and the suspect down to the police station. I had them wait in the front lobby while I got the audio/video recording equipment ready for the interview. Both the suspect and his mother decided that they didn't want to call a lawyer or have a lawyer present during questioning. That doesn't happen too often. Most suspects refuse to talk and usually want to call an attorney or have an attorney present during the interview. Most times, when the accused persons make that phone call to a lawyer, they are specifically told not to say anything to the police or answer any questions.

During the interview, I informed the suspect that we had surveillance video of him involved in an armed robbery at the variety store. I also told him that he had been positively identified as the person responsible for the robbery. I basically told him that I had no doubt he was the one who committed the crime but that I needed to know why he did it and I also wanted to know where he dumped the knife. I also asked him if anyone else was involved. At first, he said that there was no one else and that he did this by himself. After further questioning, he admitted that his older brother was also involved and that it was his idea to rob the store.

The brother was seventeen years old and according to the suspect, his sibling convinced him to do the robbery. His older brother told him that if he got caught, he wouldn't get much of a punishment because of his young age. In other words, his older brother convinced him to do the dirty work in order to save his own ass. He figured that a 17-year-old would be more severely punished than a 13-year-old boy. The suspect also told me that the knife he used was now hidden in some bushes located behind his apartment building.

After confessing to the crime, I told the 13-year-old to stand up and turn around to face the wall. I advised that he was under arrest for robbery. I patted him down and placed handcuffs on him. I escorted him to the cell block area where he was processed by the platoon Staff Sergeant. He was then placed in one of the cells reserved for young offenders. The law says that we have to keep young persons separate from adult prisoners. After placing him in the cell, I shut the door and locked it. This was the very first time in his young life that he had been placed in a prisoner cell.

As I was about to leave the cell block, he sheepishly said, *"Excuse me officer. Could you please tell my mom to bring me my pyjamas and a deck of cards?"* Can you believe it? Mr. Tough Guy walks into a variety store, pulls out a large knife and demands money and cigarettes while terrorizing the clerk. Now, all of a sudden he wants his mommy to bring him his pyjamas and some playing cards while he sits in a prisoner's cell. This 13-year-old was so naive to believe that he could actually wear his pyjamas and play solitaire while sitting in a cell right after being arrested and charged with armed robbery.

I broke the news to him and let him know that he was not allowed to have those items that he requested. In fact, prisoners are not allowed to have much of anything while being a guest of her majesty. Their shoes and belts are taken away from them because shoe laces and belts can be used to commit suicide. All property including jewellery, money and other personal items are taken from the jail birds and kept until they are released from custody. Anyway, the kid had a sad look on his face when I told him that he couldn't have his pyjamas and cards. Aw, poor thing. I guess he was going to have to sleep in his street clothes for the night. The court appearance for a bail hearing was scheduled for the next morning.

I followed up on the information regarding the 17-year-old brother. He came in for questioning and during the interview I told him what his brother had said. I made him aware that he had been implicated in the armed robbery. He denied any involvement and said that his younger brother was lying. He said he wasn't anywhere near the variety store the day it got robbed. He refused to answer specific questions and kept saying that he had nothing to do with it.

We had canvassed the area for potential witnesses who might have seen suspicious activity around the time of the robbery. One neighbour said that he was looking out his kitchen window and saw someone standing across the street from the variety store. He seemed to be looking around like he was waiting for something and then suddenly ducked behind some bushes when a car drove by. Another neighbour had observed someone lurking in the area and standing at the side of the variety store. A couple of times he peered around the corner of the building. None of these neighbours were able to positively identify any of the suspicious persons. It was dark outside and they weren't close enough to see their faces.

When I re-interviewed the 13-year-old about his brother's involvement, he recanted his original statement. That meant that he changed his story and said that his brother was not involved. He explained that they got into a big fight and argument the previous day before the robbery. He was just trying to get back at his older brother because of the argument. I didn't believe him and he was definitely covering for his older sibling. Perhaps, he was coerced or threatened into changing his statement. It was obvious that both of them were involved. The problem was that I didn't have enough evidence to substantiate any charges against the 17-year-old and the younger brother wasn't cooperating.

During the investigation, a 12-inch kitchen knife was located and seized as evidence. The money and cigarettes were never recovered. The 13-year-old was charged with robbery and possession of a weapon dangerous to the public peace. He received probation for one year. He had to write a letter of apology to the store clerk and perform thirty hours of community service work and not come within fifty metres of the victim's place of employment.

This was not the first time that the police became involved with this family, nor would it be the last. Unfortunately, these two brothers caused a tremendous amount of grief and heartache for their mother over the years. I felt bad for her because she did the best she could as a single parent. She was always cooperative with the police and I have to say that this isn't always the case when dealing with parents of wayward youths. Many times they will cover for their kids and teach the kids that the police are not to be trusted. We don't tend to get much support from these types of parents. I'm not saying that all parents behave this way. Believe me, we do have lots of good ones out there. It's just that we interact with so many of the bad ones that after awhile we get disillusioned.

CHAPTER ELEVEN

Failure In More Ways Than One

"Sex is one of the most wholesome, beautiful and natural experiences money can buy." -Steve Martin

The 40-year-old bonehead should never have made the offers. What the hell was he thinking? He apparently met the girl at a party more than a year before he was arrested and charged. According to him, they were both at a party and drinking alcoholic beverages. She ended up giving him her cellphone number. Now, I have to tell you that I'm the cop that eventually arrested this guy. I had to sit in an interview room with him and just to be clear, I know what he looked like. There is no way in hell that this girl would have given him her phone number. Even if she had consumed copious amounts of alcohol, there is no way she would have done that.

At a later date, he sent her a text message and offered to pay $100 if she agreed to have sex with him. She refused the offer and told him that she had a boyfriend. Instead of getting the hint and stopping there, what does he do? He sends her another text message and offers her $250 to have sex with him. She turned him down a second time and told him that his propositions were inappropriate. He made other offers to engage in sexual activity that included mutual masturbation and oral sex. Each time, his offers were rejected.

What a class act. Oh and did I already mention that the girl was fourteen years old? Although, the obscene text messages would have been inappropriate no matter what age she was. By now, she was extremely angry and had enough of his repulsive comments. She made it clear from the very beginning that she wasn't interested and now felt that she needed to be more assertive. The girl sent out one final message to the insufferable creep. She told him in no uncertain terms to go fuck himself and leave her alone.

So how did the police find out about this pedophile offering money in exchange for sex? Well, it turns out that the young lady forgot to delete her text messages. Then one day her mom decided to go through her daughter's phone to go over the highlights of the weekend. I guess the mother was in the habit of doing this at least once a week. Needless to say, when she saw the latest texts, she flipped out. The frantic woman made her feelings very clear. She gave her daughter a tongue lashing for exchanging text messages with this guy. Just the thought of this disgusting pervert sending sexually explicit messages to her 14-year-old child made her feel sick to her stomach.

After screaming and yelling at her daughter, mom called the guy and unleashed an expletive-fuelled outburst over the phone. She threatened to find him and remove his testicles (testes). After removing his testicles, she was going to insert them into his oral cavity and down his pharynx. She specifically said, *"I will rip your fucking balls off and shove them down your fucking throat!"* She called him almost every name you can imagine and then some. He remained silent and just listened to her screaming and yelling. After a minute, he abruptly hung up without saying a word. Now she was even more pissed off.

Surprisingly, he called her back after about five minutes. Was he calling to apologize and promise never to do it again? Was he feeling guilt and remorse? Not at all. In fact, he made mom a cash offer to have sex with him. I guess he figured that she was closer to his age so why not give it a try? He offered her

$300 to have sexual intercourse and an extra $100 for some mutual masturbation and oral sex. The poor woman blew a gasket and threatened to kill him. I really don't want to repeat the specific language that was used by mom. She was so enraged that she once again launched into a profanity-laced tirade. This weasel (no offence to the actual mammal) once again abruptly hung up after his failed attempt at an intimate relationship with the girl's mother.

So now you're thinking, mom must have called the cops right after the guy hung up on her. You would think that she reported the incident so that the police could investigate the complaint. Nope. Wrong again. After all that yelling, screaming, swearing and threatening, the mother never called the police. That's right. The incident was not reported to the authorities. Maybe she thought that she had inflicted enough verbal punishment on the guy and that there was no need to involve the cops. She might have had other plans for him. Who knows?

So, how was this finally brought to the attention of law enforcement? How was I so fortunate enough to have this incident fall on my lap? As it turns out, the sexting creep went to work one day and decided to talk about it with his colleagues. Yeah, that's right. The matter only came to light later, when the failed cellphone Romeo decided to shoot his mouth off to his buddies at work. He apparently told his co-workers that it was a classic love story. He met a girl, shared some laughs, drinks and established a connection. At the end of the night, she gave him her phone number. Nice work, Casanova! A legend in his own mind. He confessed the details of the text messages exchanged with the 14-year-old girl and the interesting phone discussion with her mother. One of his co-workers was concerned about his behaviour and did the right thing. He called the police and reported the incident. That's something that the girl's mother should have done from the very beginning.

A report was initially taken by a uniformed patrol officer. The information was then forwarded to the detective office and assigned to me. It was now my responsibility to conduct a follow-up investigation. I read over the report and couldn't believe how stupid this guy was. During the investigation, I was able to interview the 14-year-old female victim, her mother and some of the suspect's co-workers that he had spoken to.

Based on the information that I obtained, I contacted the suspect and made arrangements to have him attend the police station. He was told that I needed to speak with him in regards to an investigation that I was working on. He agreed to meet with me and about thirty minutes later, he was sitting in the front lobby of the station. I have to say, that was quick. I remember how nervous he was when he came to the police station. I brought him into the interview room and had him sit down. He wanted to know what was going on and acted as though he was very surprised about having been contacted by the police. I advised him that I was investigating a complaint regarding lewd and inappropriate text messages sent to a 14-year-old girl. All of a sudden his face turned red and he stopped talking. He was fidgeting in his chair and appeared to be uneasy or uncomfortable. I also informed him that based on the information already obtained, he was being arrested and charged with child luring. His cellphone was also seized and tagged as evidence.

> *Child luring as defined under s. 172.1 of the Criminal Code is the use of telecommunication by the accused who communicates with a person he believes is under the age of 18 for the purpose of facilitating the commission of certain sexual offences with that person. Such offences include sexual interference, sexual exploitation and invitation to sexual touching.*

The accused indicated that he wanted to speak to a lawyer. As required by law, I provided him with a list of legal aid lawyers to choose from. He telephoned one of the attorneys from the list and was able to get legal advice. Following the advice of counsel, the accused exercised his right to remain silent and refused to answer any questions. I told him that he didn't have to say anything to me but that he might be interested to hear what I had to say about the investigation and why he was being charged. After telling him a little bit about the investigation and explaining the criminal charges, he simply blurted out, *"I didn't mean it. I was only joking."* To me, that's a confession. He could have vehemently denied any involvement by saying that he didn't do it, that we had the wrong guy or that someone else must have used his phone. There was no denial, whatsoever. He was later released with a court date and conditions. I completed all follow up and arrest reports along with an information to substantiate the criminal charge against him.

He eventually plead guilty in court and was given a fourteen month conditional sentence ("house arrest") with strict terms. This was followed by three years probation. The terms or conditions included an order that he couldn't leave his home except for medical appointments, going to work or attending school. His worst punishment was that he also lost his job as a result of his stupid actions. He wasn't allowed to go to parks, community centres, schools, day cares or any other places where minors could be present. He had to abstain from alcohol and was prohibited from possessing weapons. He was also placed on the Sex Offender Registry for ten years. He was forbidden to use a computer or cellphone for the purposes of communicating with anyone under the age of sixteen.

In court, the Judge lectured the accused that if he had to serve his sentence in jail, he would suffer the harsh realities of a moral code practised by inmates where sexual offenders (particularly those whose cases involve children) would be brutally treated. Both literally and figuratively, that could have ended up being a bummer!

A little bit of advice to everyone. If you do receive unwanted texts or emails from a sexual pervert you should not engage them. Stop all communications and block their phone number or contact. You might be tempted to retaliate and show your displeasure but the best thing to do is to ignore them. If you continue to be harassed then you need to immediately report the incident to the police. Getting into a verbal slugfest with these degenerates doesn't help. Sometimes they might be emboldened by your anger or get turned on by it. They may be looking for a reaction of fear or anger and resistance just to satisfy their weird or sick sexual urges.

CHAPTER TWELVE

Is That A Gun In Your Pants, Or Are You Just Happy To See Me?

The two uniformed cops were walking the beat downtown during their 6:00 p.m. to 4:00 a.m. shift. Officers Doug and Mike were good friends and were talking about the Blue Jays baseball game that was played earlier in the day. They were also looking forward to getting together for a backyard barbecue with their families the following weekend. This particular Saturday evening started out fairly quiet and the weather was extremely hot and humid. You could see it from the sweat stains on their light blue shirts.

We were still about four years away from switching to the dark navy blue shirts (based on the LAPD uniform). Every other police department in Ontario had already switched over to the new shirts except for Peel Regional (Mississauga/Brampton) and Brantford. Don't ask me why. Wearing that damn body armour was pretty uncomfortable as well. However, the more you sweat wearing body armour, the less you'll bleed out on the streets. Or something like that. The thought of the other cops driving around in air conditioned cruisers pissed them off even more. But what could they do? It was their turn to walk the beat.

By about 10:00 p.m., the pace started to pick up quite a bit and the radio calls were coming in fairly steady. Throughout the night, patrol officers were responding to a variety of disturbances that included intoxicated persons, domestic disputes, fights, assaults and noise complaints. They also arrested a number of people for impaired driving. Just another Saturday night in the city.

It was around 12:30 a.m. and Mike had just finished writing up a parking ticket on a car that was blocking a fire hydrant. The portable radio crackled with an all-too-familiar call regarding a suspicious male hanging around in front of a bar downtown. A concerned citizen called the police to report that there were drugs being sold on a street corner near the tavern.

What else is new? This watering hole certainly had the reputation of being one of the roughest bars in town. We used to get calls for disturbances involving loud music, fights and intoxicated persons refusing to leave almost every night and especially on the weekends. The bar's liquor licence was previously suspended for serving alcohol to underage and intoxicated persons.

Anyway, the boys in light blue started making their way over to that area to investigate the complaint. When they got there, the suspicious person (if he actually existed) was gone on arrival. Sound familiar? Remember those boring and mundane calls that I wrote about earlier? They walked around and checked the back of the building but there was no one there. Occasionally, you would find some potheads smoking weed at the rear of the tavern. Officer Doug notified the dispatcher to advise that they had checked the area and that the suspicious person was GOA. They cleared the call and were about to resume foot patrol.

One of the partners suggested stopping in at the coffee shop down the street. At least there was air conditioning in there and they could cool off a bit. Sounds like a plan. Suddenly, someone jumped to the ground from a second-floor balcony located above the tavern. The jumper hit the ground, narrowly missing the two officers, and ran off on foot. The cops just looked at one another like what the hell just happened? They chased him up the street where he was finally nabbed about one block away.

The beat cops didn't know who this guy was and had no idea why he had jumped from the balcony and fled on foot. Now they had to investigate to find out what was going on. They had reasonable and probable grounds to believe that the suspect had committed a criminal offence. As a result, they detained him for questioning. Doug asked him for identification while Mike was being called by the dispatcher. The suspect was checking his pockets for his ID but couldn't seem to find it. It appeared as though he was simply going through the motions, pretending to look for his ID. Doug noticed the suspect fidgeting with the waistband area of his pants.

Officer Mike was on the radio getting some additional information from the dispatcher. An anonymous 9-1-1 caller was reporting that there was a guy inside the tavern with a handgun. He said the man pulled the gun from his waistband and pointed it at him. This was somehow related to the suspicious person call that Mike and Doug had just cleared from. He felt his heart race when the dispatcher further advised that a second 9-1-1 call had just come in regarding a male person in possession of a firearm and threatening people at the tavern. Mike was standing about ten feet away from his partner and the suspect being questioned, when he noticed the bulge at the front of the suspect's pants. This undoubtedly aroused his suspicion.

Officer Mike took quick action when he saw the man reach again at his waistband, purportedly to fish out his ID. He ran over and tackled him to the ground. A violent struggle ensued as both officers tried to gain control of the suspect and attempted to handcuff him. The guy continued reaching for something in his waistband as the officers were trying to subdue him. They punched him until they were able to gain control and snap on the handcuffs. While searching the prisoner, a loaded 9mm semi-automatic handgun was found in the waist band of his pants. Officer Mike's suspicion and quick action may have saved his partner's life. A 19-year-old from Toronto was charged with carrying a concealed weapon, possession of a weapon dangerous to the public peace, careless storage of a firearm and breach of probation.

The investigation revealed that the drug dealer had come to town to sell some crack cocaine and marijuana. He had earlier walked into the tavern and had an argument with another patron. A crowd gathered around them and he eventually left. He later walked back into the tavern and a witness reported seeing a man holding a gun in his right hand but quickly lost sight of him. The suspect apparently tried to leave again but when he opened the door to get out of a building, he noticed the two beat cops arriving on scene. He quickly retreated back into the tavern and somehow ended up on the second floor. At one point he made the stupid decision to jump off a balcony and make his getaway. This imbecile could have laid low for awhile and just waited for the cops to leave. To top it all off, none of the witnesses came forward to provide any statements to the police. That's not surprising. Nobody wanted to get involved and who could blame them?

This incident could have been a very dangerous and frightening situation for those who were inside the tavern that night. Thankfully, no one was injured or worse. Officers Doug and Mike "dodged a bullet" that night and were able to get together for their barbecue the following weekend. All's well that ends well.

CHAPTER THIRTEEN

Nothing Like A Sunday Afternoon Brawl

It was just another warm day in June and I was assigned to patrol the east end of the city. It was a sunny Sunday afternoon and so far I had investigated a couple of minor fender benders, a noise complaint and responded to a domestic dispute. Nothing too serious. It was just after 1:00 p.m. when I got dispatched to a parking complaint. Some idiot decided to park his pickup truck in front of someone's driveway.

As I made my way over to the call, the dispatcher came over the radio advising that she needed some patrol units to clear and be available for a major disturbance in progress. You could tell by the dispatcher's voice that this was serious.

Someone called 9-1-1 to report a large group of young men fighting and armed with weapons at a Colborne Street East motel parking lot. Oh yeah! Nothing like a Sunday afternoon brawl.

Just prior to our arrival, a number of suspects fled the scene but we were able to quickly apprehend several people that were still fighting when we arrived. Witnesses said that it looked like a full-scale riot. Reports from bystanders indicated that there were approximately twenty people involved in the brawl. They were armed with a variety of weapons that included crowbars, copper pipes, baseball bats, a broken broom handle, some two-by-fours and possibly a knife.

Pepper spray had to be used to subdue a couple of these knuckleheads who were resisting arrest. One officer drew his firearm when a suspect armed with a baseball bat refused to put it down. I believe that looking down the barrel of a gun pointed squarely at his chest may have convinced him to drop the bat. Several suspects were taken into custody and the weapons were seized as evidence. All witnesses had to be interviewed.

Two of the suspects were treated at the scene by paramedics for minor scrapes, cuts, and bruises. Thankfully, no one was seriously injured. Most importantly, none of the responding officers were injured. It's a miracle that, with all those improvised weapons, no other persons were hurt in the brawl. Although, I have to give credit to our swift and heavy police response. As a result of our quick actions, we may have prevented this melee from becoming a life-threatening incident. We could have ended up with bodies lying on the asphalt parking lot of the motel. We were there in less than a minute and most of the thugs fled the scene when they heard police sirens. It definitely could have been a lot worse.

We checked with the hospital to see if anyone had walked into the ER with suspicious injuries. Hospital staff advised that no one had come in but that they would keep an eye out and notify us. Suspects involved in these types of situations will sometimes drive themselves or their buddies to a hospital for medical treatment, depending on how badly wounded they are.

Our investigation revealed that earlier, a Toronto man unexpectedly met a former girlfriend in downtown Brantford. What are the odds? More importantly, why do they all end up coming here? Anyway, the man allegedly grabbed the young woman in a sexual way as they walked together. She struggled and escaped. The man followed her back to the motel, where friends of the 16-year-old Cambridge girl confronted him about the sexual assault. He was outnumbered and decided to leave.

He later returned with a group of friends from Toronto and the fight began. I should have renamed this chapter, *"The Out-Of-Towners Prequel."* I'll provide some background information for those of you who may not be familiar with my first book. I had written a chapter entitled, "The Out-Of-Towners." It explained that street gang members from the Greater Toronto Area (GTA) were coming to our city to sell illicit drugs. Over a period of time, we had a number of shootings connected to these thugs from out of town. The shooting incidents occurred about fourteen years after the infamous Sunday afternoon brawl. It's obvious that some of the GTA gang members were here long before the gun violence started.

As a result of the parking lot brawl, a 22-year-old Toronto man was arrested and charged with sexual assault, causing a disturbance by fighting, possession of a dangerous weapon, assault with a weapon and breaching probation. Five others were charged with possession of a dangerous weapon, assault with a weapon and causing a disturbance by fighting. The accused persons included two 19-year-old males from Toronto, a 21-year-old male from Brampton, a 23-year-old male from Toronto and a 22-year-old male from Brantford (the odds are that there had to be at least one Brantford guy involved). One of the 19-year-old males was also charged with breaching probation.

Ah, the good ol' days when fists, baseball bats, knives, crowbars, chains, steel pipes and broom handles were used during street fights. Nowadays, you can bet that guns will be involved and shootouts will occur. I guess it's a lot easier to just pull out a gun and squeeze the trigger. Who the hell wants to swing a baseball bat or steel pipe at someone or get involved in a fistfight? Too much work.

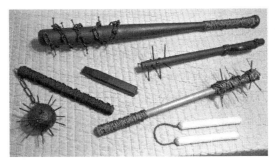

NOT the weapons used in the Sunday brawl

CHAPTER FOURTEEN

Batman Needs Assistance

I was assigned to the Uniform Patrol Section and had just started my shift at 7:00 a.m. The dispatcher called me over the radio and interrupted my Tim Horton's coffee break. I was instructed to immediately attend the front lobby of the police station. Apparently, there was a special assignment waiting for me. As I drove to the station, I was racking my brain trying to figure out what this was all about. A special assignment? Sounded very exciting and intriguing. It definitely sounded much more exciting than routine patrol. You are probably not going to believe this. You'll just think that I've made up this story just to fill up the pages and make the book more interesting. After all, it's been pretty boring so far. Right? Anyway, back to my story.

When I arrived on scene, I was surprised to see the Batmobile parked right in front of the police station. I parked my cruiser and walked into the front lobby. I was utterly astonished to see Batman standing at the front desk talking to one of our officers. I say standing but he was using crutches as he leaned up against the counter. He looked exhausted and worn out. A few other officers were struggling with someone in the reception area. As I got closer, I realized that the person they were trying to subdue was one of Batman's most well-known enemies, Catwoman.

Catwoman is an expert thief who has crossed paths with Batman on many occasions. However, she is an inconstant villain and occasional ally to Batman. She became more of a dangerous anti-hero rather than a villain. I do know that over the years, Batman and Catwoman have had a complex love–hate relationship. So, was this a domestic violence issue or had Catwoman been caught committing some other crime? After all, we know that she is a professional burglar and jewel thief. Either way, I was about to find out.

It turns out that Batman had apprehended Catwoman during a high-end jewelry store burglary. She broke into the store and filled up a large bag with higher quality fine jewelry before attempting her getaway. Batman had been notified by the security company because there weren't any police officers available to respond to the burglar alarm. Batman saved the day! He dropped into the jewelry store like a knight in shining armour. The Dark Knight that is. The Caped Crusader.

Batman interrupted the break and enter in progress. He loudly announced to the feline felon, *"Sorry, kitty-cat, but it's game over!"* She dropped the bag of jewelry and hissed loudly. He quickly took a couple of steps back. Her eyes were fixed and unblinking with her legs slightly bent as she crept steadily towards Batman. It appeared as though she was ready to pounce with her claws. Instead, she became quite flirtatious with the Caped Crusader and he slowly fell into a trance. Catwoman is known for using flirtatious behaviour or seduction to gain the upper hand or to catch someone off guard.

She was meowing and purring while moving very carefully towards her prey. She slowly wrapped her arms around his neck, pulling him closer for a kiss on the lips. The pussycat's lips were almost touching his when he suddenly looked away and quickly snapped out of the trance. He finally realized what was happening and the fight was on. Catwoman is well-versed in martial arts and can really whip and kick some ass. They engaged in some intense hand-to-hand combat. Both of them put up a valiant fight but there could only be one winner, Batman!

The Caped Crusader removed the bat-cuffs from his utility belt and proceeded to place the restraints on Catwoman. He escorted her to the Batmobile and drove her down to the police station. Several officers waited in the parking lot for the Batmobile to arrive. When they arrived at the station, Catwoman remained feisty and aggressive. She yelled out that she could *"smell pork" a*nd threatened to *"kick some bacon ass."* They had to drag her into the front lobby as she hissed, spit, clawed and kicked at the police officers. I had walked into the station as they continued to struggle with her until they finally got her under control.

My job was to take over the arrest from Batman and place Catwoman into police custody. I would then be responsible for laying the appropriate criminal charges and completing the paper work. I also had to conduct videotaped interviews with the Caped Crusader and the feline felon. Batman was given some crutches to use. He had apparently sprained his ankle while trying to capture Catwoman. He was encouraged to seek treatment at the hospital after being interviewed. He was quite reluctant to visit the ER but told me that he would go.

I asked Batman to remove his bat-cuffs from Catwoman's wrists so that I could apply my own police issue handcuffs. I had a heart-to-heart talk with her and explained that I needed full cooperation while switching the cuffs. I further stated that if she didn't follow my instructions, I would have to notify the OPP canine (police dog) to come down and pay her a visit. As you know, most cats and dogs do not get along for a variety of reasons. I reminded her that cats and dogs have an innate dislike of one another, meaning the two will naturally fight until they draw blood or one retreats. I gave her a few seconds to think about what I had just said. After a brief moment of silence, I said to her, *"You've got to ask yourself one question. Do I feel lucky? Well, do ya, pussy?"* I could tell that Catwoman was in no mood to go one-on-one with police dog Rover and she promised to behave herself during the handcuffing procedure.

As a result, Catwoman was placed in police custody for the burglary and theft. She didn't put up any resistance but she did try to get frisky with me. The frolicking feline was meowing and purring while being handcuffed. The stolen jewelry was also seized and tagged as evidence. She was held for a bail hearing that would take place at the courthouse, the very next morning. Under the Criminal Code, you have the right to a bail hearing within twenty-four hours of being arrested if a judge is available, or as soon as possible if one isn't. On the morning of her scheduled hearing, the pussy prowler was brought to court and appeared before a Provincial Court Judge.

The assistant Crown attorney presented the allegations against the accused to the court. The Crown and defence lawyer presented legal arguments and evidence as to why the accused should or should not get bail. After listening to both sides, the judge stated that he was not going to pussyfoot around and the request for bail was denied. As a result, Catwoman would have to be locked up until her next court appearance.

Unfortunately, the feline felon somehow managed to escape custody while incarcerated at the Brantford Jail. How she was able to do this is a complete mystery. Did she squeeze through the bars? Did she plan and execute the purrrfect jailbreak? No one knows for sure. Catwoman has proven to be very elusive to law enforcement personnel and an arrest warrant still exists to this day. A fugitive task force was created in order to track down and capture Catwoman. This unit consists of specially trained police officers known as the Pussy Posse. Hopefully, she will be found and arrested in the not-too-distant future. That's my story and I'm sticking to it.

The original 1966 Batmobile
What did you expect? A photo of me arresting and handcuffing Catwoman?

Police officer arrests Catwoman

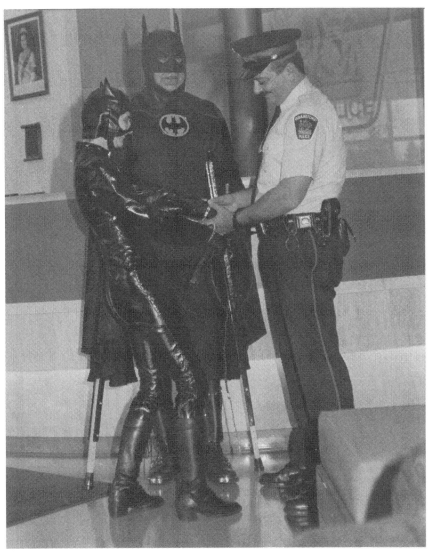

Batman stands by on crutches as Police Officer Rick DiGiandomenico handcuffs Catwoman. The feline felon was earlier apprehended by the Caped Crusader during a botched jewelry store burglary and theft. Batman sustained a sprained ankle during the incident. The officer smiles as Catwoman appears to exhibit some flirtatious and seductive behaviour.

CHAPTER FIFTEEN

One Fatal Night

"Good-bye, Dad. See ya later." Those were the teen's last words to his father that evening. He never came home and died in a car accident just a few hours after he left the house to go hang out with some friends. The teen was a passenger in a car with three of his buddies. Just after midnight, the car was speeding southbound on Birkett Lane when it veered off the roadway and slammed into a tree. The 17-year-old driver was killed instantly. A 16-year-old passenger was rushed to hospital but was pronounced dead some time later. Two other teens were also taken to hospital. One was listed in critical condition while the other was listed in serious condition.

A passerby happened upon the scene just minutes after the accident occurred. He stopped his vehicle and got out to render assistance. He saw one of the injured teenagers lying on the ground beside the crumpled car. The good Samaritan told the accident victim to stay completely still and hang on. He said that he was going to go call for an ambulance and that he would be right back. The man got into his vehicle and drove to the nearest house he could find. He started pounding on the front door of a residence and calling for help. This was before cell phones were prevalent in our everyday lives. The home owner was frightened and called 9-1-1 to report that a man was banging on her door and shouting that there was a bad car accident up the road. The caller told the 9-1-1 operator that the guy kept yelling something about people being badly hurt and that someone may have been killed.

The police radio crackled to life and the voice of the dispatcher broke the silence of an otherwise quiet night. I was immediately dispatched to the call along with two other patrol units. The only information we had was that a motor vehicle collision had occurred on Birkett Lane involving multiple victims and a possible fatality. We also received information that EMS had been notified and were responding to the accident scene. When I responded to the call, I activated my emergency lights and siren. As I arrived at the crash scene, I knew it was going to be a bad one. I observed the heavily damaged vehicle that had slammed into a large tree. I could also hear one of the injured teens screaming for help. Two ambulances quickly arrived on scene and the paramedics attended to the injured victims.

I approached the driver's side of the vehicle and observed a male victim who appeared lifeless. I could see that he had severe facial injuries and a large gaping wound across his forehead. I also observed what appeared to be brain matter oozing from the head wound. There was blood everywhere. I checked for a pulse but couldn't find one. It was an all-too-familiar death scene because I had been in this situation before. I felt helpless. There was nothing I could do. You would think that after a while, you would get used to it but you never do. You have to control your emotions and act professionally. You do your job but you never get used to it. The paramedics came over to examine the victim and confirmed that he was dead. The 17-year-old driver sustained fatal injuries resulting from impact with the windshield and steering wheel.

At the time of this tragic accident, the roads were wet and clearly there was some speed involved. Accident investigators from the Traffic Section were also called out that night. The specially trained officers attend all traffic collisions involving fatalities or serious injuries. We cordoned off the area around the scene of the accident. Part of the investigation would involve seizing the vehicle and looking into whether there may have been any mechanical failures. An officer from the Forensic Identification Section was also called out to photograph the accident scene. This included taking photos of the vehicle involved in the fatal collision and the body of the deceased.

We also had to wait for the Coroner to attend the scene to examine the body and pronounce death. The Coroner is responsible for determining the cause of death, which sometimes can be done at the scene, but in most cases will require a post-mortem for further examination. Once the Coroner released the scene, a body removal service was called in to transfer the remains of the deceased 17-year-old. Autopsy results revealed that in addition to the head injuries, the young driver had also sustained severe chest and abdominal injuries due to the impact of the collision. This also caused massive internal bleeding. Motor vehicle accident injuries tend to be much worse for drivers and passengers that are not wearing seat belts at the time of the accident. Airbags are not enough to protect you in the event of a crash and are designed to work with seat belts, so buckle up.

When a car hits a very large tree while travelling at a fast speed, it is remarkable that anyone could survive. How could the crash have happened? Was the driver intoxicated? Using drugs? Reckless? Inexperienced? The test results showed no alcohol or drugs in the driver's body. This corresponded with the account of the two surviving boys. The survivors also claimed that the driver was not reckless but did admit that he was driving real fast. Speeding was certainly a factor, just how fast could not be accurately determined. During the investigation, potential witnesses were encouraged to come forward with any information. It was imperative to interview and take statements from anyone who might have seen the accident. This could assist the investigators in determining the cause of this fatal collision.

I can only imagine the parents of those dead teenagers waking up to the most horrific news of their lives. I can't help thinking about it. Such dark and sombre thoughts are not just a product of my job environment but also a product of being a loving dad of three children. I once read an article from the New York Times called, *'Teenagers and Cars: A Deadly Mix.'* The article mentions tha*t,* 'the joy of a newborn's arrival is followed by the stealthy creep of a deep-seated parental dread that lurks most ominously behind a lightly piped request: *"Mom and Dad, can I have the car keys?"*

What actually breaks (and bursts) in the body during a crash? First, depending on the impact of the crash, you can probably expect a broken collar bone. In a higher speed impact, you start to break ribs. The more energy you're absorbing on the ribs, the more ribs you'll break. Once you've broken enough ribs, the chest loses its structure and you start to impact upon the lungs. If a lung is punctured, air leaks into the space between your lung and the chest wall. As the amount of air in this space increases, the pressure against the lung causes it to collapse. That's just one of the first injuries that happens in a high-speed frontal crash. I think you get the idea. Let's leave it at that.

Thankfully, two of the teens survived their injuries. Although, the road to recovery would be long and hard for them. Both teens would require extensive physical therapy after their surgeries. As a result of this horrendous single-vehicle accident, two teenagers were dead and two emotionally scarred for life despite recovering from their physical injuries. Treatment and therapy for someone involved in a serious motor vehicle collision today spans far beyond the physical. Those who have sustained emotional trauma after a car accident can attest to it, but now insurers have fallen in line to recognize the necessity of clinical counselling for mental health therapy. After all the years that have passed, I hope that the two survivors are doing well today.

Statistics show that the risk of a motor vehicle accident goes up when teens drive with other teens in the car. At least 48% of teen drivers and passengers aged sixteen to nineteen years who died in passenger vehicle crashes in 2019 were not wearing a seat belt at the time of the crash.

Parents: Make sure you and your young driver are aware of the leading causes of teen crashes and injuries:

- *Driver inexperience*
- *Driving with teen passengers*
- *Nighttime driving*
- *Not using seat belts*
- *Distracted driving*
- *Drowsy driving*
- *Reckless driving*
- *Impaired driving*

"Please buckle up, pay attention, follow the rules of the road and for God's sake, SLOW DOWN. Is that too much to ask?"

CHAPTER SIXTEEN

Can't Get Enough of those B&Es

I am not talking about bacon and eggs. For those of you who may have missed chapter three, B&E stands for Break and Enter. Also known as a break-in or burglary. If you read my first book, you would know that B&Es in progress were my favourite calls to respond to. Nothing like catching criminals in the act of breaking into someone's home or business. The victims of this type of crime suffer far more than lost possessions when their home is broken into. There can be a lasting effect on the whole family and they often feel violated as their home is no longer a safe haven. Victims can sometimes experience a profound sense of loss when items of sentimental value are taken or damaged and a loss of privacy, knowing that someone has gone through one's personal belongings.

The majority of our B&E calls are the ones where the break-in has already happened and the criminals are long gone. If the homeowner (victim) intends to file an insurance claim, a police report will be required. They may also want advice from police regarding home security measures. The patrol officers submit the incident reports and then it's up to the detectives to conduct followup investigations and hopefully solve these crimes. Unfortunately, quite a few of these break and enters often go unsolved. If somebody breaks into a house and nobody sees anything, we have absolutely nothing to follow up on. That's basically it. Sometimes we'll receive a Crime Stoppers tip that may help us to solve these cases. Most homeowners don't keep track of product serial numbers, so finding common electronic devices once they're sold at pawn shops and returning them to their owners is nearly impossible.

Every once in awhile we do get that call about a break & enter happening right now (in progress). Maybe a silent alarm has been activated or an eyewitness, such as a neighbour has spotted some suspicious activity. Hopefully, someone will call 9-1-1 and we'll be able to swoop in to make the arrest. Of course, it's not always that easy. There are times when we may have to get involved in a foot chase or even a vehicle pursuit in order to apprehend the criminals. Sometimes we arrest them while they are still on the premises, without having to exert ourselves in a chase. This often occurs when we have the house or building surrounded and the criminals have nowhere else to run. Of course, there is always the possibility that the B&E suspects might be armed with weapons. But that's another story.

It was early Sunday morning just after 3:00 a.m. when the 9-1-1 call came in to the dispatch office. You guessed it. It was a B&E in progress. At that particular time of day I needed something to pick me up. Something to get the heart pounding and the adrenaline rushing. After all, it was earlier in my career and I was still relatively young. The house was located up in the north end of the city not far from the intersection of Balmoral Drive and Woodlawn Avenue. The person calling 9-1-1 said that the homeowners had gone away for the weekend.

I arrived on scene and positioned myself at the front of the house. My backup officer arrived and proceeded to the rear of the property. We decided to wait for another patrol unit to get there before going in. The officer covering the backyard area radioed the dispatcher and advised that he had located the entry point. He reported that the sliding patio door had been forced open and believed the suspects were still inside the residence. The dispatcher acknowledged the update and assigned additional units to the call. Seconds later, the same officer was back on the radio yelling that three male suspects took off running westbound through backyards. I ran towards that area to assist the officer.

As I got closer, I observed two of the suspects running in behind some houses further down the street. I quickly approached the area on foot and then observed the same two suspects running out from between two houses. I drew my firearm and ordered them to get on the ground and place their hands behind their heads. I advised them not to move. I radioed my position and my back up officer came over to my location and assisted me in arresting the suspects. I handcuffed a 23-year-old male while the other officer handcuffed a 16-year-old male. I advised both that they were under arrest for break and enter. I also informed them of their right to counsel (the right to speak to a lawyer).

I then heard someone yelling, *"Stop! Police!"* I turned around and observed a third male suspect running down the sidewalk as one of the officers pursued him on foot. The suspect bolted across the street and ended up in a backyard of one of the houses. The foot chase continued as he ran across the yard and jumped over the back fence. Talk about your heart pounding and the adrenaline rush. To be honest, I was also getting a little tired. The suspect jumped over several fences and we briefly lost sight of him. We searched one of the backyards using our flashlights and found him hiding under a deck. He was ordered at gunpoint to come out from underneath the deck and to get on the ground with his hands behind his head. After a lengthy foot chase down the street, through yards and over fences, we finally had the suspect lying face down on the ground in handcuffs. The 17-year-old was under arrest for break and enter. He was also given his right to counsel.

We then had to search the residence that was broken into and make sure that there were no other suspects hiding inside. Additional officers arrived to assist in the search because we didn't how many suspects were involved. The three stooges that were under arrest, refused to say anything or answer any questions. They were invoking their right to remain silent. During the search, no other persons were found in the residence. I went back into the house to survey the crime scene while two of the other officers transported the prisoners to the police station.

Before going in, I observed that the sliding glass patio door had been pried open. The locking mechanism was broken and the screen had been removed and damaged. I entered the residence and found that the house had been completely ransacked. The living room couch was overturned and a table lamp had been knocked over. The kitchen drawers and cabinets were open. The bedrooms had been ransacked. Dresser drawers had been pulled out and the contents dumped onto the floor. I also noticed several jewelry boxes and pieces of jewelry on the floor. I found a window that was wide open in the master bedroom and noticed that the window screen had been removed and damaged.

I entered the garage and found a television set on the ground near the garage door. I also located a stereo receiver that was left on the roof of a 1985 Pontiac Bonneville 4-Door Sedan. The driver's side window was smashed and I could see a large amount of shattered glass on the driver's seat and the floor of the car. The vehicle was registered to the homeowner. The ignition wires had been pulled out of the steering column in an attempt to hot-wire the car. As a result, the steering column and ignition switch were damaged. It was obvious that the intruders were going to steal the car and take off with the stolen property. Unfortunately for them, their plan was foiled when the police arrived.

I radioed the dispatcher and requested that a Scenes of Crime Officer (SOCO) attend the residence to photograph and examine the crime scene. The burglars had placed some stolen property in the back seat of the vehicle. We found more in the trunk. All items were seized and tagged as evidence. Seized property included a VCR, two television sets, stereo receiver, CD player, microwave oven, jewelry (necklaces, bracelets and rings), $400 in cash, bottles of liquor and a case of beer.

It was the next door neighbour who had called the police to report the break-in. He informed me that the homeowners were away for the weekend but had no idea where they were staying. I was unable to locate any telephone numbers for family members or relatives. After the scene was examined and documented, I secured the residence and left a note for the homeowners informing them of the break and enter investigation. I also left a business card with my contact information.

I spoke to the witness living next door to the house that was broken into. He provided me with a statement. He told me that he had arrived home shortly before 3:00 a.m. and was in his bathroom washing up. He looked out of his bathroom window after hearing some noises. He saw a silhouette of a person with bushy dark hair standing on his neighbour's patio in the backyard. The outdoor flood lights were not on at the time. He thought it was strange because his neighbour would normally leave the lights on all night. It was rather mild outside and the bathroom window was open. The witness overheard someone saying, *"oh shit, I just seen somebody looking at me."* After hearing this, he ran to the kitchen phone and called police. He stayed on the phone with the dispatcher until we arrived. I thanked the eagle-eyed witness for noticing the suspicious activity around his neighbour's property and for calling the police right away.

The Scenes of Crime Officer and I transported the seized property back to the station and placed all items in the evidence lockers. I completed the General Occurrence/Arrest reports pertaining to the Break and Enter incident. A separate Motor Vehicle Report was completed for the attempted theft of the car. An Information for Charge was submitted for each of the accused persons. I also requested a bail hearing for all three of the prisoners. Criminal charges included:

- break, enter and theft
- attempted theft of motor vehicle
- possession of break-in instruments

The 23-year-old was also charged with breach probation. He had a criminal record with convictions for break and enters, thefts, assault and impaired driving. When I arrested him, he was on probation for a previous break and enter and had to abide by the conditions or rules set by the probation order.

Probation rules are designed to protect other members of the public from reckless behaviour and to ensure a degree of accountability to keep the offender from falling back into negative patterns of behaviour. Well, it certainly didn't work with this particular offender. He managed to avoid a jail sentence for his last conviction and promised to behave himself and stay out of trouble. In reality, he didn't give a crap about the probation order and continued to commit crimes. He displayed his arrogance and basically thumbed his nose at the criminal justice system.

Residential break and enters are fairly common and happen more often than many people would think. Most criminals who commit break-ins do it to support their ongoing drug habit. While the majority of citizens take adequate measures to protect their homes, many underestimate their safety requirements. Sliding glass doors are prime targets for criminals looking for an easy entry into a home. They are often blocked from view, left unlocked and have an overly simplistic locking mechanism. The locking mechanism on most sliding glass doors are easy for a burglar to bypass. Often, the lock is nothing more than a mere latch that hooks into the door frame when the door is shut.

Most sliding glass doors are located on the back of the home and hidden from view. The seclusion gives criminals full cover and plenty of time to break-in undetected. People often forget to lock the back sliding glass doors. It's also a good idea to insert a metal or wooden bar along your sliding door's bottom track. Ultimately, no entry point, lock or barrier is completely foolproof. Like I've said before, an even better idea is to install a security system in your home. It's money well spent and will give you greater peace of mind.

Police nab three people

Three males, trying to carry away stolen goods from an Allensgate street house, were nabbed by police early Sunday.

Witnesses watched as the three broke into the back door of the home at 3 a.m. They fled when police arrived but were captured after a foot chase.

The thieves had ransacked the home and were planning to load possessions into a car in the garage, police said.

Two male teens, who can't be identified under the Young Offenders Act, and 23, of were charged with break, enter and theft, attempted theft and possession of burglary tools.

Newspaper article from the Brantford Expositor: October 1992

There can be a lasting effect on the whole family and they often feel violated as their home is no longer a safe haven.

Victims can sometimes experience a profound sense of loss when items of sentimental value are taken or damaged and a loss of privacy, knowing that someone has gone through one's personal belongings

CHAPTER SEVENTEEN

Watch Out For Flying Beer Bottles

It was certainly a hot and muggy night. You know that sort of night where you'd like to kick back and relax with an ice cold brew. Beer that is. Except that I couldn't because I was on duty working the afternoon overlap shift from 6:00 p.m. on Friday until 4:00 a.m. on Saturday. I was assigned to foot patrol in the downtown area. I got back to the station for my 10:00 p.m. dinner break. At 11:00 p.m. I went back on patrol and drove around in the big blue police van which is a large vehicle also known as a prisoner van or paddy wagon. That was the usual routine when you were walking the beat. You were on foot patrol for the first four hours of your shift. After dinner break you would be assigned to patrol in the police van for the remainder of the shift. Your foot patrol partner would be assigned to do dispatch relief from 10:00 p.m. until 1:00 a.m. When the dispatch relief duty was completed, you would pick up your partner at the station and resume patrolling together in the van.

It had been an extremely busy weekend with calls for service piling up. After all, it was summer time and it was hot. At the beginning of our shift, we were advised that there was an outdoor rock concert taking place in the west end of the city. We were told that this was a private party and that they were expecting up to two thousand young people to attend the concert. Sounds like a lot of fun. Four rock bands were expected to play at the event. The music had started at around 5:00 p.m. on Friday and the party was expected to continue into the early morning hours of Saturday. Wow! That's a long time to party. A hot and humid night with a couple of thousand young people consuming alcoholic beverages and the possibility of some of these young people using illicit drugs. What could possibly go wrong?

We received multiple noise complaints after the concert began. Officers had responded to several incidents in the area that included a vehicle break-in, a fight, underage drinking in public and impaired driving. Noise complaints from local residents came from as far as three miles away from the venue. People that lived in this community were angry and frustrated. They had every right to be pissed off. They called police and demanded that the music be turned down or shut down. As a result, this prompted us to close down the concert. Shortly after midnight, fifteen police officers in several cruisers arrived at the concert location and moved in to close down the big party. We also had to turn away people trying to attend the concert and disperse large crowds milling about the parking lot. Some property damage occurred when destructive concert-goers became hostile following an announcement that the concert would be shut down because of excessive noise complaints.

We noticed a large group of about thirty people loitering in the parking lot and blocking vehicles trying to get out. One of the officers approached the disorderly youths and asked them three times to disperse. They argued that they had a right to stay and refused to leave. The group was quickly becoming increasingly loud and belligerent. They were shouting obscenities and threatening the officer as he tried to get them to leave the area. There was one guy yelling something in a manner suggesting he was trying to incite the other youths. An officer approached the intoxicated agitator from behind and tried to take him by the arm, telling him he was under arrest for causing a disturbance. The suspect yanked his arm from the officer's grasp. Another attempt was made to take him by the arm and shoulder. He pushed the officer in the chest and squared up in a combative stance, facing the officer.

    I went up behind the guy and grabbed his right arm while the other officer took a hold of his left wrist and upper left arm. We brought him to the ground and pinned him down. While on the ground, he continued to resist arrest as we were handcuffing him. A hostile crowd started to form around us and several of his drunken buddies attempted to interfere with the arrest. They were preventing us from handcuffing our prisoner and tried to pull him away from us. Fortunately, more officers arrived to assist us and we were finally able to take the agitator into custody. Two of the young hooligans that tried to interfere with the arrest were also apprehended and taken into custody. A few of them got away just before the other officers came over to assist us.

    The group continued yelling profanities and causing a disturbance. Extra officers were called in to restore order, with some officers having bottles and other objects thrown at them. One of the officers put a warning out over the police radio to, *"Watch out for flying beer bottles."* I got to see a few of those bottles sailing through the air that night. I came to the conclusion that I would rather drink a bottle of beer instead of getting hit in the head with one. As the old saying goes, *"I'd rather have a bottle in front of me than a frontal lobotomy."* Or *something like that.*

At one point, I observed that more of the rowdy teens and young adults were coming from the direction of the concert venue and moving towards the police. One guy ran up to an officer and started yelling profanities. He got up real close to the officer's face and the officer shoved him backwards and ordered him to leave. The guy refused to leave and once again, approached the officer and was yelling, *"Fuck you!"* He assumed a fighting stance, clenched his fists and postured his body as if he was going to attack. The officer was in fear for his safety and reacted without hesitation. He used his forearm to strike the suspect in the face. The young man fell to the ground face-down, and was ordered to put his hands behind his back. He was handcuffed and taken into custody.

All of a sudden, a bottle was thrown from the crowd. It was quickly followed by a hail of debris: bottles, cans, stones and broken-off pieces of concrete. As a result, we had two of our police cruisers damaged during the disturbance. A door on one of the cruisers was damaged by a beer bottle. The other had a window smashed when a couple of hoodlums jumped on the vehicle. By this time, more officers arrived on scene and were helping to bring the crowd under control. Several troublemakers were arrested for various criminal offences.

The offenders, who were also consuming alcohol, ranged in age from sixteen to twenty-one. Charges included assaulting police, resisting arrest, cause disturbance by fighting, obstruct police and possession of narcotics. We placed them in the big blue prisoner van (that vehicle sure came in handy when we had multiple arrests) Whenever that big van pulled up to a scene, everyone noticed. The good news is that no one was seriously injured during this large disturbance. In fact, the Ontario Provincial Police (OPP) had also been notified and placed on standby. Thankfully, they were not needed. Although, it was good know that they were available to respond if required. Oh well, just another fun night in the city.

CHAPTER EIGHTEEN

Is It The Heimlich Or The Hind-Lick Manoeuvre

I wasn't present when this incident happened. I can only go by what I was told. I thank my lucky stars I wasn't the one to witness this horrible and repugnant sight. I'm not sure that I can even get through writing this story but I will try. It's not a scene you think you would see as a police officer but in this line of work, anything is possible. As I've said before, you have to be ready for anything. Unfortunately, there was one young officer who was there and I'm sure he ended up having to see a therapist. Nothing had prepared him for what he was about to walk into. I heard that he had experienced some nightmares but eventually got over it and is doing well today.

It was during the day shift and the 21-year-old rookie officer was in the middle of writing some reports at the station. He had just come back from investigating a three car motor vehicle accident involving a hit and run driver. There were also some minor injuries but nothing too serious. At one point he decided to take a quick washroom break. You know that feeling. You're so focused and busy working that you forget to go the washroom. At some point you realize that you just can't hold it in anymore. I guess I'm getting a little sidetracked. So, the officer decides to take a washroom break and heads over to the locker room. This was our new police station that had a locker room with showers and a washroom. We even had a fitness room at the new station.

The rookie stepped out of the report room and walked down the hallway towards the locker room. He passed the exercise room on his left side and waved to a couple of off-duty officers who were working out at the time. He pushed the locker room door open and walked in. He could hear the shower running as he made his way to the washroom. While standing at the urinal, he thought about being in a nice warm shower after a good workout. He could almost feel that spray of water splashing on his face in the hot, steaming shower.

All of a sudden he woke up from his daydream when he heard some loud gasping and grunting sounds coming from the shower area. He also heard a couple of hard slaps. He moved away from the urinal and quickly washed his hands. The strange sounds continued and he looked around the corner to see what the noise was all about. He laid eyes on something so appalling and hideous that he began to feel nauseous. His heart started beating really fast and all he wanted to do was get the hell out of there. It must have felt like the walls were closing in.

Now remember, I wasn't there but I did talk to this young officer several days later. By now, the story had made its way through the grapevine. I thought it would be a good idea to go talk to the eyewitness and hear it straight from the horse's mouth. Of course, I was just being nosy. So, I'll do the best I can to describe what the rookie cop observed when he peeked into the shower area. This is how he explained it to me. There they were. Two naked men standing in the shower. Both men were off-duty police officers who had just finished their workout. That's not unusual at all. That's what showers are for.

What was unusual in this case, was that the bigger and much heavier man was standing behind the average-sized man with his arms wrapped firmly around his waist. When comparing their body sizes, these guys reminded me of the famous comedy duo of Laurel and Hardy. The heavyset individual appeared to be making thrusting movements while the other person was bent slightly forward. Both bodies were wet and the rookie could hear suction sounds along with the grunts and gasping. The terrified officer who had observed and heard all of this, quickly turned around and headed for the locker room door. He couldn't believe what he had just seen and didn't know what to do. Just as he was about to step into the hallway from the locker room, he heard one of the men yelling out his name and telling him to come back. He said he needed some help. The poor officer was thinking, *'what does he mean by help? What the hell do these guys want me to do?'* He told himself not to panic and went back in. First he was told to shut off the water. Then he was asked to help lay the victim on his back. It appeared he was losing consciousness and they needed to perform CPR.

The young cop was actually relieved to hear this. *'Oh, good. It's just a naked guy needing CPR. Thank God,'* he thought to himself. When he first noticed the two guys in the shower, it must have looked as though there was some sort of hanky-panky going on. I don't blame him at all. During the Heimlich manoeuvre, you are standing behind the person (who is bent slightly forward) with your arms wrapped tightly around their waist while delivering inward and upward thrusts to the abdomen. If you're both in the nude and standing in a shower, someone could mistakenly believe that the "victim" is being penetrated from behind. I apologize for the graphic description.

As it turned out, the guy was choking on a couple of throat lozenges or cough drops. So, it wasn't what the rookie cop initially thought it was. He hadn't walked in on two naked men engaged in sexual activity. Instead, one of the off-duty cops was performing the Heimlich manoeuvre on his workout partner. The big guy saved the other guy's life on that fateful day while showering. He had a couple of throat lozenges in his mouth when all of a sudden he went into a really bad coughing fit. The medicated candy got sucked back into his throat, causing him to choke. Just before they were about to lay him on the shower floor, the rotund hero delivered one final abdominal thrust which finally caused the lozenges to be expelled from the victim's airway. Thankfully, he never lost consciousness and CPR was not required.

This was a teachable moment. A couple of takeaways here that can help you in the future. Never have more than one cough drop or candy in your mouth at the same time. Especially when you're working out or showering. More importantly, never shower alone. Always make sure that there is someone there with you because you never know when you might need the Heimlich manoeuvre or CPR done to save your ass. By the way, the Heimlich manoeuvre should never be confused with the Hind-lick manoeuvre.

On a serious note, Dr. Henry Heimlich, thoracic surgeon and creator of the famed manoeuvre that saves people from choking to death, died at the age of 96. In his own words, he best explains the profound nature of this triumph:

"What makes the Heimlich Manoeuvre particularly special is this: it is accessible to everyone. Because of its simplicity—and the fact that it works when performed correctly—just about anyone can save a life. Each of us can save the life of a stranger, a neighbour, a spouse, or a child. And it can happen anywhere—in restaurants, homes, ballparks—you name it. You see, you don't have to be a doctor to save a life. You just have to have knowledge and the instinct to respond in a crisis."

-Dr. Henry Heimlich

Just imagine these two men in a shower without any clothes on.
What would you think? Exactly!

CHAPTER NINETEEN

Like Something You Would See On TV Or In A Movie

It was just a few weeks before Christmas. As we all know, the Christmas season is busy. The hustle and bustle of this time of year is considered to be just part of it. Many songs have been written and Andy Williams sang it best. It's the most wonderful time of the year. The endless shopping and parties. Christmas is a time to be enjoyed. It is the time to be with family and close friends. However, let's not forget the true meaning of Christmas. We get so busy and distracted that it's easy to lose focus on the real reason for the season.

The incident began at 5:30 p.m. on a Saturday. The police dispatcher received a 9-1-1 call about a man sitting in a parked car trying to kill himself. The guy ran a hose from his exhaust pipe to the inside of his vehicle. In other words, he was trying to commit suicide by carbon monoxide poisoning. When police arrived, the car was gone and one of the officers radioed the dispatcher to report that the vehicle and person were GOA. A description of the vehicle and occupant was broadcast to all units. Officers were advised to be on the lookout for this car and occupant.

The vehicle was later spotted by a patrol officer travelling on Brant Avenue. The officer pulled in behind the car and began to follow it. The cruiser's roof lights were activated and the dispatcher was notified. The officer blasted the horn a couple of times to get the driver's attention but he ignored it and continued to drive. He quickly turned right onto a side street and headed towards Grand River Avenue. He turned right again and finally decided to pull the vehicle over and stop.

The officer updated the dispatcher and got out of his cruiser. He walked up to the car and as he got closer, he observed the driver turning toward him in the seat, holding a handgun with his right hand, pointing it across his chest and out of the driver-side window. The officer drew his firearm and quickly distanced himself from the vehicle. He ordered the suspect to put down his weapon.

The suspect put the vehicle in drive and accelerated towards the officer. He pointed the gun at the officer as he drove towards him. The cop fired two shots and hit the vehicle. The driver took off while the officer ran back to his cruiser. He notified the dispatcher and advised that he was in pursuit of the vehicle and that the driver was armed with a gun. The officer also advised that he discharged his weapon when the suspect drove toward him.

This guy was now becoming a threat to the community. Not only was he driving dangerously but he was also armed with a gun. The chase ended up in front of our hospital's emergency department and now the suspect was in a standoff with the cops. He was ordered to come out of the vehicle with his hands up but he refused. Six police cruisers had blocked the suspect's vehicle and he had nowhere to go. The suspect did cause some damage to a couple of the police cars by hitting them with his vehicle as he tried to get away but finally realized that he wasn't going anywhere. Now he was armed with a gun and refusing to surrender.

The hospital emergency department was placed on lockdown but people were allowed to leave the building through alternate exits. First he tried to gas himself to death and now he was yelling at the cops to kill him. Was this going to be a suicide by cop? The officers took cover but could see that the suspect was still waving the hand gun around. A short time later, the officers were able to get the guy to calm down. With guns drawn, they conducted a high-risk takedown of the suspect as he finally surrendered. He was safely removed from his vehicle and a hand gun was seized by police. The 25-year-old man was charged with dangerous operation of a motor vehicle, failure to stop for police, possession of a weapon for a dangerous purpose, pointing a firearm, driving without a licence and taking a motor vehicle without consent. The accused was also held in custody and ordered to undergo a psychological assessment. This guy definitely had some mental health issues and needed professional help.

This was a bizarre series of events that included gunshots, a car chase and a standoff with police. A witness described the scene as like something you would see on television or in a movie. Another witness praised police for *"doing a great job"* in quickly ending the standoff. The suspect's gun was determined to be a replica. An extremely realistic replica, identical in virtually every area except that it was incapable of firing bullets. It was a fake gun.

What some people might not realize is that when police officers find a gun, they treat it as if it's real until they're absolutely sure it isn't. A replica firearm is classified as a weapon when it's used in the commission of crime. If a person uses it in a robbery or threatens someone with it, they will be arrested and charged. That's probably the best outcome because being arrested is a lot better than being killed. Getting killed would be a lot worse. If a person goes around brandishing an imitation firearm, they may very well get themselves shot by the police.

It happened in our city many years ago. I had only been on the job for about three years. It was my platoon working that Saturday night in October. Two of my coworkers were involved in this tragic incident. The officers were dispatched to a domestic violence call. A woman had been assaulted by her estranged husband. The officers went to the suspect's home to question him about the assault. He pulled out what appeared to be a Colt Python .357 Magnum revolver on a police officer after being told he was under arrest. When the man refused to drop the weapon, he was shot in the chest and subsequently died of his injuries. When they examined the suspect's firearm, it was discovered that the gun was a toy, a replica, and not the real thing at all. To the officers, the replica looked exactly like the real thing and they had no choice but to defend themselves.

About seventy-five minutes after the standoff ended outside the hospital, the dispatcher received another 9-1-1 call. Officers were dispatched to a restaurant parking lot on King George Road. The caller stated that a young man had a gun tucked in his belt. The gun had also been pointed at several people coming out of the restaurant. Officers quickly arrived on scene and observed a van pulling out of the parking lot. They conducted another high-risk takedown of the vehicle and occupants. Four teenagers were arrested and two replica handguns were seized. Nobody got hurt and nobody got shot.

At the beginning of this chapter I wrote about the hustle and bustle of the Christmas season. Unfortunately, not everyone thinks of it as being the most wonderful time of the year. For many people, it's not. The *"holiday blues"* – feelings of loneliness, loss or isolation that psychologists say can heighten during the holidays – affect people with or without mental health disorders. It can be brought on by grief or illness, spurred by the loss of a job or the end of a relationship, and compounded by the stress and pressure of the holidays.

The 25-year-old involved in the standoff tried to kill himself or get himself killed that day. He made the right decision to give it up and surrender. He could have come out of the vehicle and pointed the gun towards the cops. I can guarantee you that if he had done that, he would have been shot by the officers. Something in his mind told him not to do it. Maybe he wasn't ready to die that day or maybe he just wanted to live and get the help that he needed. All's well that ends well.

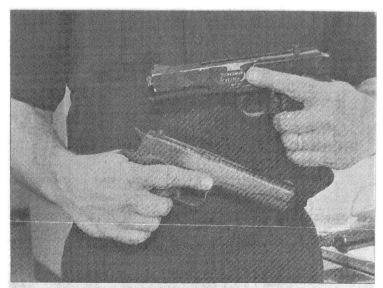

A police officer demonstrates the startling similarities between a replica gun (top) and a Colt .45 semi-automatic. *Expositor Photo by Kyleigh Buryta*

Replica gun on the right next to a semi-automatic handgun on the left

Police officers have only a couple of seconds to react when confronted by a person with a gun and don't have time to assess whether it's real or fake

CHAPTER TWENTY

One Of My Last Investigations Before Retirement

I was working on some follow-up reports in the detective office when I received a faxed report from a police officer in another jurisdiction. It was an occurrence report detailing a complaint by a parent in regards to possible abuse and/or neglect of his son. The father of this boy had noticed some lesions, blisters, burns and other marks on his son's lower back, buttocks and legs. Although the complainant and his family lived in another municipality, his son attended a special needs school located in our city.

I reviewed the report that was faxed to our office and determined that I needed to attend the school and speak with the Principal. I obtained a written statement from the Principal regarding his internal investigation into the injuries allegedly sustained by the young boy while in the care of the school. The Principal told me that he had interviewed a few of the staff members who worked closely with the student and would have had an opportunity to see any injuries to his body. The staff members apparently didn't see any such injuries. They told the Principal that this kid seemed to be in good spirits and didn't show any signs of discomfort.

I contacted the Sexual Assault and Child Abuse Unit of the other police department and requested that they do a videotaped interview with the complainant (father of the boy) regarding his son's injuries. I also requested that they send me a copy of the interview, along with photographs and medical reports. I later received a package from the other Police Service containing two DVD copies of the interview, along with an interview synopsis, medical report, injury photographs and a copy of the occurrence report.

After reviewing the material, I contacted several employees at the school and made arrangements for each one of them to come in to do a videotaped interview. The employees that I would be interviewing, all had regular and significant daily contact with this particular student. Some of the staff members told me that they should have been able to see any types of injury while toileting and/or bathing the boy. However, they didn't see or have any knowledge of any marks, blisters, burns or other injuries on the body of this child while he was in their care at the time. They told me that had they observed any such injuries they would have immediately reported them to their supervisors and Principal. In fact, they would have sought immediate medical attention for him. I also asked each of the staff members if they would consent to a polygraph test ("lie detector test"). They all said that they would definitely agree to take the test because they had nothing to hide.

I interviewed the student's primary care giver and Educational Assistant. She would have been the last to toilet the kid before he went home for the weekend. She confirmed that she didn't see any injuries on the body at that time, or earlier in the week. She also explained that the young boy often rocked back and forth quite vigorously, whether on a chair or physiotherapy ball. That would have been quite painful for him if the injuries had been there during that particular week. He had also been in a chlorinated pool on two occasions that week and he would have experienced quite a bit of pain if there had been a rash or lesions and blisters. She further stated that even sitting would have been painful and staff members would have noticed or recognized some kind of pain response and/or crying from the boy. The primary care giver was interviewed again at a later date and she reiterated that no injuries were observed on the body of the boy. She further stated that if she had seen these injuries, they would have been reported, documented, photographed and attended to by a medical professional.

As part of my investigation, I also reviewed the medical report completed by a doctor who had seen the boy when he was back home for the weekend. The doctor examined the patient and identified skin rashes, diaper dermatitis and eczema. In the doctor's report, there was mention of possible burns, trauma from sitting/rubbing on the toilet seat and possible abuse. The report further stated that the lesions on the buttocks appeared to be three to four days old. However, the information was noted to be largely inconclusive.

I also reviewed the videotaped interview conducted by the other Police Service with the father of the boy. Based on witness credibility and witness corroboration, I determined that there was no evidence to indicate that school officials were responsible for the injuries reported on the body of this child. If these injuries really existed, the staff members at the school would have been able to see them and would have reported them. You would think that someone other than the kid's father would have seen these types of injuries if they were there. Why is it that only the father and the doctor saw them and no one else? There was no evidence of any collusion or conspiracy, nor were there any inconsistencies or contradictions in the various accounts provided by the school employees.

I contacted the complainant (boy's father) by telephone and provided him with information regarding the investigation and its conclusions. I asked him why he hadn't seen the injuries reported on his buttocks and back until the following day after he had picked up his son at the airport. He told me that he and his son were tired when they got home that evening and that he quickly changed his son's diaper without seeing his condition.

I advised him that I didn't find any evidence to indicate that any of the staff members at the school were responsible for his son's injuries. There was no evidence that these injuries were caused deliberately or by neglect. I told him that the employees were all interviewed and that they had all denied any involvement or responsibility for the injuries reported by him. In other words, there wasn't a shred of evidence of any criminal wrong doing by the staff at the school and the investigation was going to be closed. Needless to say, dad was not impressed or satisfied with the results of my investigation.

Before I officially closed the case, I had to tie up some loose ends. I contacted the assigned caseworker at the Children's Aid Society and advised them of the results of my investigation. I also contacted the caseworker with the Children's Aid Society located in the boy's hometown. She indicated that the original doctor who examined the boy had now concluded that the marks on his body were more likely caused by a severe diaper rash as opposed to a chemical burn. This conclusion was supported by the Child Protection Team at the Children's Hospital in that jurisdiction. They also found that the rash could have developed over time or spontaneously depending on a variety of factors. I forwarded this information to our local caseworker that I had previously spoken to. After completing all necessary reports and documents, the investigation was closed.

I mentioned that the father/complainant was not happy with the results of my investigation. Almost a year later, he attended our police station and spoke to another officer. He was demanding that the investigation be re-opened because he had some new evidence. The officer forwarded a report to the Criminal Investigation Section. One of our detectives reviewed the additional information provided by the complainant and he also read over my earlier reports. After reviewing all of the information, the detective concluded that there was insufficient evidence to re-open the investigation at that time. Dad was still not satisfied and said that he was going to file a complaint against our Police Service.

A review of the police investigation was conducted and it was determined that as the principal investigator, I had performed my duties with diligence and care. I had reasonably concluded that there was no evidence to support the laying of criminal charges against any staff member at the school in relation to the injuries sustained by the young boy. At all times, my investigation statements, reports and related findings were reviewed and approved by my commanding officer.

The review also found that I was an experienced officer and had conducted hundreds of investigations over my career, including allegations of child abuse. I also spent considerable time in charge of the Vice Unit which is now known as the Child Abuse and Sexual Assault unit. I also had the benefit of substantial training courses, seminars and workshops during my career. These have included training in sexual assault investigation, general investigation training, major case management, youth crime and street gang investigations.

The final report indicated that my investigation was reasonable and that the Police Service or myself should not be held liable. There was no finding of any wrongdoing or negligence. In other words, the investigation of the boy's injuries was done properly and professionally. A high-ranking executive officer (Inspector) within our Police Service, thanked and praised me for the work that was put into this investigation. I truly appreciated it.

This is the comment from the police commander that was forwarded to me:

> *Rick,*
>
> *Thank you for your professionalism. It was very apparent when you were going through the investigation as to how important this particular case was to you. The investigative interest that you took in trying to determine the extent of the injuries that this boy suffered were apparent.*

As you can see, police officers are always under intense scrutiny or as I like to say, *"under a microscope."* I do believe in police accountability and responsibility. Cops have the power or authority to take someone's life or take away someone's freedom (arrest and put in jail). So, there should be accountability and I understand that. Nowadays, police officers do feel more scrutinized than ever. In Ontario, the courts have also now allowed claims for negligent investigation if law enforcement fails to act reasonably in conducting an investigation. If this results in an injury and falls beyond the normal bounds of basic discretion, this could lead to civil liability for the law enforcement officer.

CHAPTER TWENTY-ONE

One Child's Horrific Memories

A warning that the following story contains information that some readers may find disturbing.

By the time this investigation had been assigned to me, I had already worked on quite a few of these disgusting cases. They were definitely not my favourite investigations but someone had to speak up for the young victims and advocate for them. In reality, it was the victims who had to speak up. I would be the one responsible for putting all the information and evidence together for the criminal proceedings. It's not just the cops involved in helping these victims. You have the social workers, mental health professionals, medical staff, and prosecuting attorneys. Although it's a teamwork approach, it's the police involvement that gets the wheels of justice moving. Sometimes the justice system is swift and sure. Other times, the wheels of justice grind too slowly.

Investigating these incidents can be very frustrating. If we decide not to lay charges, it doesn't mean that we don't believe the victim. As police officers, we often encounter a number of reasons for not being able to pursue these cases like not having enough physical evidence to prove the charges in court. The criteria for criminal prosecutions is quite stringent and sometimes, despite a full and truthful disclosure by a victim, the required evidence may not meet the standard set forth by the courts and the victim's complaint may not result in charges. The direction of the investigation depends on numerous factors. The police officer's role is to collect the evidence and determine if there are reasonable and probable grounds to lay charges. The police officer may request a crown prosecutor review the file to provide a legal opinion. The crown prosecutor will provide opinion about likelihood of conviction which plays a factor regarding if charges can be laid or not.

I contacted the victim's mother and scheduled a recorded interview with the victim. In the interview, I asked her to describe everything she remembered about the sexual assaults. I explained the importance of being very detailed and specific, even if talking about these incidents made her feel uncomfortable. Being as honest and detailed as possible would help me in the investigation of her case. The interview was videotaped for court purposes. At first, the young victim was embarrassed to talk about what happened. I had to reassure her that she was not at fault and was not responsible for what happened to her. After the interview, I continued with my investigation, including contacting the suspect. I also notified the girl's mother to let her know that I had contacted him. For victims, knowing when the suspect is being contacted by police is important to them. The victim's family always appreciates being updated on the status of the investigation.

As it turned out, the young girl came to live with her 39-year-old biological father and the abuse started almost immediately. The last time this incestuous pedophile had seen his daughter was when she was about three years old. She was now eleven years of age and she had no memory of him. There had not been any contact between the two of them until now. She was having some problems and her mother encouraged her to contact her father through Skype. Her daughter had been exhibiting some behavioural issues both at home and at school. Mom thought that a change of scenery would be good for her daughter. She decided that the young girl should finally meet her father and spend time with him. Eventually the mother and daughter, who were residing in another jurisdiction, went to visit the biological father at his home for a week. The girl was then sent back to her father's residence the following summer.

Just a few day after she arrived, her father began inappropriately cuddling and touching her. He then escalated the abusive behaviour by forcing his daughter to smoke marijuana, drink alcohol and watch pornography while he exposed and touched himself. He forced her to watch while he masturbated in front of her. He also bribed and pressured her to allow him to take explicit photos of her. This loathsome pervert gave his 11-year-old daughter a vibrating dildo for her birthday. The victim also disclosed that on several occasions, her father came into her bedroom at night, undid her nightdress, kissed her and touched her breasts. When I questioned him about this, the suspect told me that he had gone into his daughter's bedroom to kiss her goodnight and turn off the nightlight. He denied touching her inappropriately.

His behaviour continued to escalate and he told his daughter that he wanted to have oral sex and sexual intercourse with her. When she rejected this suggestion, saying that he was her father, he told her to think of him as a boyfriend. He used the excuse that because he had not been involved in her life, it would be okay for him to act like a boyfriend rather than a parent. This is how he tried to justify his actions to her. He persisted, and for the next two months subjected her to oral and vaginal sex. The father had sex multiple times a week with his daughter. It bothers me to think that this innocent girl had come to stay with her father that summer so that she could get reacquainted with him and perhaps have him come back into her life.

During intercourse she would say, *"No, I don't want to and it hurts."* She cried while pleading for him to stop doing this to her. He didn't care and told her to be quiet. He threatened his daughter several times and warned her that if she told anyone, he would kill both her and her mother. At some point, she gave up resisting because it was easier to accept what was happening to her. The almost daily sexual abuse only ended because the father was caught in the act by the victim's older half-sister. She walked into the bedroom and found the father performing oral sex on the victim, who was passed out from alcohol.

During my recorded interview with the accused, he claimed he was also the victim of molestation as a child by his own uncle. He told me that what happened to him years ago did not justify what he did to his own daughter. By the end of the interview he had admitted to sexually abusing his daughter. The suspect was arrested and charged with multiple counts of sexual offences that included sexual assault, sexual interference, sexual exploitation, invitation to sexual touching and incest. He was also charged with uttering death threats. The accused was held in custody for a bail hearing.

Speaking about how such alleged abuse went undetected, the Crown attorney argued that the defendant was clever and projected himself as a father figure when there were other people around. He added that, during this time, the abuse took its toll on the victim and she started losing weight and vomiting. He said that the sexual assaults became more aggressive until it finally stopped when the victim's older half-sister caught the sexual predator in the act of abusing his young daughter. The court heard from the half-sister, who testified that at one time, she had seen the girl sitting on her father's lap with his hands inside her pants.

The accused had been arrested and charged with sex offences in the past. He had a previous conviction for the sexual abuse of another young girl. The Ontario Court of Justice sentenced the accused to five years in prison after he plead guilty to sexual assault, incest and sexual interference for repeatedly raping his 11-year-old daughter. He was also registered as a sex offender. The Judge noted child victims and their families rarely achieve closure in cases such as these. *"There's coping, there's managing, there's recovering — but there's no closure,"* he said. He also commented that the young girl was traumatized after being *"robbed of her innocence"* by her father.

What I also found to be disturbing is that the girl's mother knew about her ex-husband's previous sexual assault charges and conviction. And yet, she still allowed her daughter to go and live with this convicted child rapist. Did she know about the incestuous activities? During my interview with mom, she told me that although she knew about his past, she never thought he would sexually abuse his own daughter. In my opinion, the mother should have gone to prison as well.

CHAPTER TWENTY-TWO

Murders in South Simcoe

I struggled trying to decide whether or not I should write this chapter. All the details haven't come out yet because there is still an ongoing investigation being conducted by the Special Investigations Unit (SIU). Right now, the details of exactly what happened are not absolutely clear. Hopefully, we will get more information as time goes on or whenever the SIU investigation is completed. The funeral of the two police officers will take place tomorrow in the City of Barrie, Ontario. One officer was young enough to be my son. The reason why I had second thoughts about writing this chapter is because at this precise moment, colleagues, friends, family and relatives of the deceased officers are still grieving. They are going through an unimaginable period of intense, raw and painful emotions. I feel somewhat uncomfortable writing about it while this is still happening. It's not like this incident occurred many years ago. It was just last week that the two cops were shot and killed. I thought about it and decided that this is one way for me to honour these two police officers. When people read my book, I want them to know that both men gave their lives to protect their community.

This horrendous murder of two police officers did not happen in my jurisdiction. However, I do have a slight connection to that particular part of Ontario. Every year, my wife and I used to take the kids for some skiing, snow tubing and other fun activities while we stayed at a resort located just north of Barrie. Innisfil is the actual community where the murders took place. The town is situated right next door to Barrie and along the western shore of Lake Simcoe. We also used to enjoy summer holidays and outlet mall shopping in that area. The community is policed by the South Simcoe Police Service.

The only information that I have about the incident comes from media reporting (online news sites and TV reports). I really don't know how accurate the information is and we will obviously know much more at a later time. From what we have been told so far, two officers with the South Simcoe Police Service were fatally shot inside a home during a confrontation that also left a 22-year-old suspect dead. The slain officers were identified as Constable Morgan Russell, 54 and Constable Devon Northrup, 33. Russell had the opportunity to retire three years ago but chose to keep working in the job he loved.

The officers had been dispatched to a residence in this small community of about forty thousand people. The homeowner requested assistance with a family member. Apparently, a grandmother had called 9-1-1 at about 8:00 p.m. that evening and was asking that her grandson be removed from her home after causing a disturbance. Originally this was not a gun call because there was no mention of any weapons in the house as police responded. As a patrol officer, I remember attending so many calls involving unwanted persons causing problems. Sometimes it would happen in a private residence and other times it happened in a public place. This call was different.

Police officers are dispatched to these types of incidents so frequently that they could become quite complacent and let their guard down. Officers have to keep in mind that there are no routine police calls because any one of these could get you seriously injured or killed. Yes, even the boring and mundane calls that officers deal with. I'm not saying that this is what happened here. I wasn't there and I don't know. That is just an opinion that I have and I know that there are many officers that would agree with me. This is not to find fault with anyone. It's just a reminder to stay vigilant in anything that you do in your life. It's good advice for everyone. Not just cops. Stay alert and always be aware of your surroundings.

Reports indicate that the 22-year-old grandson was smashing items inside the home after a family dispute and had gone downstairs to the basement. A police source stated that the officers were ambushed. Gunfire erupted and the two officers were struck by the suspect who, sources say, pulled a sneak attack. Apparently the gunman was hiding behind a door in the basement. They didn't have a chance. Neither Constable Russell nor Constable Northrup had drawn their firearms when they were fatally shot. Both officers were murdered in cold blood.

From what I understand, a third officer had also responded to the disturbance call. The cop killer died after an exchange of gunfire with the third officer who was not injured. Both wounded officers were rushed to the hospital but unfortunately, neither survived. The suspect was armed with a Soviet-design SKS semi-automatic rifle. This weapon is capable of firing ammunition that can penetrate police soft body armour. In other words, a bullet resistant vest would not save an officer from this type of weapon. Northrup and Russell are the third and fourth police officers to be killed in Ontario in the last month. The deaths of these four officers serves as a stark reminder of the dangers of policing. Just yesterday, an RCMP officer was stabbed to death in the province of British Columbia.

A police official stated that the joint funeral for the two South Simcoe police officers will be a significant event and unlike anything the city has ever seen. Police officers from across North America will be in attendance. Some people question why police funerals are such big events with thousands of uniformed police officers marching through the streets. When you think about it, an attack on a police officer is also an attack on our society. It affects everybody, not just the policing community. It has an impact on society as a whole. The badge represents something much bigger than the officer who wears it or the Police Service that issues it. It represents our community and all its citizens. It's more than likely that anyone who kills a police officer, doesn't respect the laws of society or even society itself.

Constable Morgan Russell   Constable Devon Northrup

CHAPTER TWENTY-THREE

The Midnight Shift

I was in the parade room just before midnight as I prepared for duty. I was assigned to uniform patrol on the night shift, starting at 12:00 a.m. and ending at 8:00 a.m. It was the middle of the week and I was hoping for a quiet shift. Parade is another name for Roll Call. This is where police officers are given their assignments and are briefed on any serious or major incidents that have occurred since their previous shift. The primary method of disseminating roll call information is through the review of the daily bulletin (the log) from the last time the shift worked. The log consists of a computer printout that contains all incidents recorded within the last twenty-four hours. This log review will encompass information related to safety issues, recent arrests and crimes, and any other information that the Staff Sergeant (Platoon Commander) or

Sergeant deems to be necessary and pertinent. Any new routine orders, directives or patrol memos will be read to the group, and, if necessary, discussed and clarified.

'Parade' for officers on the night shift

On this particular night, the Staff Sergeant highlighted some of the calls for service that were listed in the daily log. He read out information in regards to missing persons and suspects wanted on outstanding arrest warrants. He made us aware of certain hot spots of criminal activity and told us to keep an eye out in these areas that were experiencing an increase in certain crimes. In particular, we were told to be on the look out for commercial break and enters and thefts from vehicles. We were advised to focus our attention in the areas that were getting hit pretty hard with car break-ins. Well, I certainly got lucky that night. So, I might as well get right into the story.

Just after 4:00 a.m. I observed a male person tampering with the window of a car parked at the rear of one of the apartment buildings, located in my patrol zone. I was driving an unmarked vehicle and had turned off the headlights. I made a quiet approach while driving slowly towards the back of the building. Upon seeing the suspect, I immediately stopped the cruiser and radioed the dispatcher to let them know my location. I got out of my unmarked vehicle and approached him. When he saw me coming toward him, he ran and jumped over a fence. I requested assistance and provided a description of the suspect.

He was a white male who appeared to be about nineteen to twenty-one years of age. Approximately six feet tall with a heavy build and weighed about 200 lbs. He was wearing a dark coloured toque, black ski jacket and black track pants. I ran after him but he suddenly disappeared from my view. I continued to search the area with my flashlight. I had a feeling that he might be hiding somewhere close by. A short time later, I observed the same guy at the rear of another apartment building located close by. You would think that he would have been scared off the first time and would have gone into hiding or run home. Nope, not this guy. There he was, tampering with the window of a second vehicle parked behind this other building.

You have got to admit that this guy either had the balls or the stupidity to keep going. If at first you don't succeed, try, try again. Some criminals are dumb but they can be very persistent or tenacious. This thief in the night was not going to give up and was very determined to break into a vehicle. I guess I might have been a nuisance to him or perhaps a thorn in his side. I approached him and identified myself as a police officer. He said he lived near by and then started to run away. Now, why would he run away? The chase was on and I managed to catch up to him in the backyard of one of the houses located on the north side of the street. At that moment, I could hear the other police vehicles making their way into the area.

He resisted as I attempted to place my handcuffs on him. I was unable to control him and he broke away from my grasp, jumped a fence and ran westbound on Helen Avenue and then northbound on Mount Pleasant Street. I gave chase, yelling at him to stop but he ran even faster to get away. One of the police cars was heading down Mount Pleasant Street and coming right towards us. The officer drove onto the sidewalk to block the suspect's escape. That didn't deter him as he quickly turned and continued to run towards the back of one of the houses. We chased him into the backyard and cornered him. He had nowhere to go.

I told him that he was under arrest and ordered him to get down on the ground but he refused to comply. My partner and I approached the suspect so that we could handcuff him. He tried to run but we managed to grab him by his shoulder and upper body and forced him to the ground. He didn't like that and started cursing and shouting obscenities at us. He continued to resist violently, flailing his body around and kicking. During the ensuing struggle, the suspect managed to kick my partner in the stomach as he yelled out, *"You're not fucking arresting me!"* While trying to restrain him, he was extremely uncooperative. He tucked both arms under his body to prevent us from handcuffing him.

We ordered him to stop resisting and to put his hands behind his back but he refused to comply. At one point we were able to get control of his left hand and place one cuff on. The suspect continued to hold his right arm underneath him, and physically tried to keep us from pulling it behind his back. A short period of time later, we were able to pull his right arm from under him and take him into custody. We all ended up with some minor bruises and scratches. The suspect was handcuffed and as soon as we got him back on his feet, he continued to scream and yell profanities at us. He refused to walk to the police cruiser and told us that we would have to drag him to the car. So, we did. He also appeared to be under the influence of a narcotic. I couldn't smell any alcohol on him but he was definitely high on something.

Once we got him up to the side of the patrol car, we searched him and found a large screwdriver, a pair of pliers and a plastic baggie containing several pieces of hashish, individually wrapped in aluminum foil. They were all found in his coat pockets. We tried to place the suspect in the back seat of the police vehicle. We managed to partially get him inside the car but the suspect brought up his legs in an effort to prevent us from closing the door. Once inside the car, the suspect was thrashing around, making the car rock and shake. He was also screaming and kicking at the interior of the car door and window. Then he began hitting his head against one of the back windows. As a result, he sustained some cuts and bruises on his forehead. He later accused us of causing those injuries. This guy was insane and I was concerned that he would fracture his skull and/or break the window. So, we decided that we were going to hog-tie the suspect for his own safety. Fortunately for him, he must have tired himself out and stopped being violent. He calmed down and actually fell asleep on the way to the police station. I guess that working nights must have been too exhausting for him.

Myself and other officers went back to check the parking lots behind the two apartment buildings. We found that some vehicles had been entered. On one of the cars, the suspect tried to use a large screwdriver as a wedge to pry the window from its frame. The door lock was also damaged. That was the vehicle that the suspect was standing beside when I first pulled into the lot. I found another vehicle with the front passenger side window smashed and the interior ransacked. I observed the glove compartment was open and the contents were strewn about the front passenger seat. A pickup truck was found with the driver's side door slightly ajar and the glove box and centre console open. I also observed that the interior light was on. Some of the entered vehicles had been left unlocked by the owners.

    Unlocked vehicles provide easy pickings for thieves. It seems like a simple message: lock your house, lock your car, secure your property. People are either forgetting or just can't be bothered to secure their property. Some just don't care. But why make it easy for the criminals? Vehicles are sometimes left not only unlocked but with the keys inside. Some people will actually leave their keys in the ignition. How stupid is that? When you do this, you are basically saying, *"please take my car."* You might as well put a big sign on the windshield to advertise a free vehicle giveaway. You might get away with it for awhile but why take the risk? People have also been known to leave wallets and purses in their vehicles. It's a real shame.

CHAPTER TWENTY-FOUR

Not-So-Honorable Mentions

I would like to briefly mention a couple of interesting things that I do remember. These are not stories that can fill several pages of the book but definitely worth mentioning. They are more like vignettes or anecdotes about some strange or humorous situations. A mixed bag of odds and ends. Mostly odd.

I remember a young father bringing his 3-year-old son to the police station to report that his child had been sexually abused. I interviewed the father and asked him to explain in detail. He said that on two separate occasions, he took his son to the bathroom so that he could get him to poop. Both times, the father became very anxious and upset after taking a look at his son's poop. According to dad, the poop was shaped like a penis. It's because of this, that he surmised that his 3-year-old boy had been sexually assaulted. I'm not making this shit up! Kind of funny but sad at the same time. He even offered to collect a stool sample and bring it to the station for me to look at. I told him we would not require that as evidence. It was obvious that dad was experiencing some type of mental health crisis. I hope that he was able to get the help that he needed. In his own mind, he actually believed everything that he was saying.

Before the end of each shift, the patrol officers are required to gas up their vehicles before driving them back to the police station. The cars can then be ready for the next shift. There was one particular officer, who shall remain anonymous. When you got into a car that had just been returned to the station, you would automatically have known that this particular officer had been driving that vehicle. The interior had a distinct odour, if you know what I mean. I'm not talking about the fragrance of cologne. This officer was known to be quite gaseous. The first time you smelled it, you might say something like: "SWEET MOTHER OF GOD!!! What is that smell? As you got used to it, you would just say, oh I guess Bob was in this car today. Oh well, at least it's clean. Maybe Bob didn't quite understand that gassing up the car only meant filling the tank with gasoline.

During an arson investigation, I had been assigned to conduct surveillance on a house. I was in plainclothes and sitting in an unmarked police vehicle. A young man living in this house was suspected of starting fires. Several suspicious fires had occurred in this part of the city. We had received a Crime Stoppers tip about this guy. We suspected it could be him because he had a history of committing arson. Years earlier, he was arrested for setting some garages and sheds on fire when he was just eleven years old. They couldn't charge him at the time because he was underage. Now it sounded like he was up to his old tricks again.

The arsonist was recently targeting front porches of homes, vehicles and backyard sheds. He had to be stopped before someone was injured or killed. Our plan was to watch him, follow him around and hopefully catch him in the act. I parked my vehicle just far enough from the house so that I wouldn't be spotted. We had another plainclothes officer watching from the other end of a side street. I was in radio contact with the other surveillance unit at all times. For awhile, there was absolutely nothing happening. Then all of a sudden, I see the suspect coming out of the house.

He walked down the driveway, stood there and looked around for a moment. Then he went back into the house. What a disappointment. We knew this guy was getting ready to strike again because it had been several days since the last fire. It was just a matter of time. For some arsonists, setting fires is like an addiction or sickness. I decided to have a closer look with my binoculars and noticed that all the lights were out in the house. I thought it was a little early for him to go to bed. I looked up towards the upper level of the two-story home. I noticed a quick movement on the rooftop. I focused my binoculars and was startled to see the suspect perched on the rooftop and staring right back at me with his own binoculars.

I was watching him at the same time that he was watching me. I guess you could say that we were doing surveillance on each other. Unfortunately, my cover had been blown and I radioed my surveillance partner to make him aware of the situation. I decided it was best to leave the area while the other officer remained on his surveillance post for about another hour. Nothing happened that night. However, I am happy to report that the suspect was eventually arrested and charged with multiple counts of arson. He even did some jail time.

One morning, I was supervising a team of officers that had been assigned to conduct a door-to-door canvass of a downtown apartment building where a murder had taken place during the night. Our job was to contact the tenants in the building and interview them to see if they had heard or seen anything suspicious. When we arrived on scene we noticed that a television news crew had setup their cameras and were about to start videotaping. They saw us getting out of our vehicles and immediately pointed the cameras towards us. Detectives in suits and police officers in uniform looking very professional. As a cohesive group, we walked across the street in unison while carrying our clipboards and notebooks. We made our way up the stairs leading to the front doors of the building. The camera crew continued to videotape the scene for the six o'clock evening news. Yes, we were going to be on television.

There we were, approaching the double door entrance to the building looking very official and authoritative. Another officer and I pulled on the door handles at the same time. We pulled again and nothing happened. We pulled one more time and my stomach sank when I realized that these doors were locked. Apparently we were at the wrong side of the building. So, we quickly turned around and walked back down the stairs while the camera crew kept the video rolling. It was a little embarrassing and we tried not to laugh.

Anyway, we had a job to do and off we went to the other side of the building. This time we found the doors that were not locked and easily made our way inside. Too bad the cameras weren't there when we opened those doors. The good news is that the camera crew and news reporter must have felt bad for us. As a result, the video clip of the Keystone Cops trying to get into the building was never aired on the evening news. We didn't make the cut. Thank God!

During the mid 1990's we were dealing with some bizarre incidents involving women being assaulted. These occurred mainly in the downtown and west end areas of the city. There was this guy going around and attacking women with shaving cream. He stalked his victims, sneaked up on them and smeared their faces and hair with shaving cream. He then ran away, laughing like a maniacal villain. These incidents went on for several months before the 21-year-old perpetrator was finally caught. No one was injured from the attacks, or at least, not physically. The victims were all females between the ages of fourteen and twenty-nine.

The *Shaving Cream Attacker* confessed to his cream crime spree after being identified by one of the victims. He was sentenced to sixty days in jail and three years probation. Although nine women were attacked, he only admitted to assaulting seven victims. He was either being untruthful or he simply lost count of his victims. However, there is the possibility of a copycat criminal who might have been responsible for two of the assaults. Either way, the incidents suddenly stopped after the Foam Felon was arrested. He apparently suffered from impulse control disorder.

EPILOGUE

'*Ontario's Most Dangerous City*'. I know there are people out there (maybe you) who might be thinking or saying, *"Here goes Rick again talking about how dangerous Brantford is. He just keeps perpetuating that fear. Why is he trying to make this city look bad?"* The truth of the matter is that I really only used that particular title so that I could capture people's attention. I remember pitching my original idea for a book title to my son, Mark. I was going to call it, '*Policing in the Telephone City.*' His response was, *"That's kind of a boring title. You need something that will grab people's attention."* What he meant to say was that my original idea for a title was lame. He was just too nice to say it that way.

Then I remembered when Maclean's magazine ranked Brantford as the most dangerous city in the province and the eleventh most dangerous in Canada. The ranking was based on a comparison of 2006 crime statistics from cities across Canada. That's how I came up with the current title. I knew that I couldn't just call it *'Ontario's Most Dangerous City'* without some kind of credibility or validity. It had to make sense. You can't just say that a particular city is or was the most dangerous without backing it up with some factual information. At the same time, I wasn't out to prove the title of the book. This city has definitely had its highs and lows but all in all, it is a fine city to live in and raise a family. I'm sure that many communities throughout our beloved country have had their turn at being the most dangerous at one time or another.

I would like to thank my wife, Rose who took the time to proof read my book manuscript. She provided me with some valuable input and feedback. There is one issue that I would like to clarify. In chapter eight, I wrote about the mundane parts of the job. The police calls that can sometimes be boring or seemingly routine. I gave a couple of examples of 9-1-1 calls involving domestic disputes. I didn't mean to insinuate that these types of calls are mundane or boring. Family trouble or domestic violence should never be minimized or taken lightly.

I was referring to situations where the police respond to emergency calls and are unable to locate any trouble when they arrive. The calls are unfounded. Persons at the location may not want to cooperate with the cops and refuse any assistance. With these types of calls, there is nothing that the officers can do and have no choice but to leave. Sometimes, a person calls 9-1-1 and it turns out that they were mistaken about what they actually saw and heard. Don't worry if your suspicions turn out not to be an emergency. You won't be charged or fined.

    Citizens should always be encouraged to report suspicious circumstances to the police. If it's suspicious to you, it's worth reporting it to 9-1-1. Help from the public is always appreciated because police officers can't always do this job alone. Sometimes, people are reluctant to call 9-1-1 because they believe their call will be a burden or unnecessarily tie up police resources. They might also believe that the police will criticize or admonish them, if the call turns out to be nothing at all. As long as you have reason to believe that there is an emergency, you won't be in trouble with the police. Most cops prefer an unfounded call instead of having to respond to a serious incident.

    However, police officers will not tolerate anyone who deliberately misleads emergency services or calls 9-1-1 as a prank. Like those kids, mentioned in chapter eight, who got into trouble for calling 9-1-1 as joke. As we all know, all emergency services are affected by false emergency calls. False emergency calls divert emergency services away from people who may be in life threatening situations and who need urgent help. This can mean the difference between life and death for someone.

I would like to thank you for taking the time to read my book. I sincerely appreciate it. I hope that you enjoyed it and were able to gain a deeper understanding of this chosen profession. Just after I published my first book, a retired colleague of mine sent me a congratulations email. He stated,

"I just finished reading your book. It was quite enjoyable and certainly a flashback for me. I was surprised by how much things have changed, and also how little things have changed."

His email message reminded me of the phrase that was coined by French writer Jean-Baptiste Alphonse Karr, *"plus ça change, plus c'est la même chose."* In English it means, *"the more things change, the more they remain the same."*

Some things have certainly changed over the years. There are a lot more guns on the street that the police have to worry about and a lot more gang activity. When I started on the job many years ago, coming across guns during a traffic stop used to be rare. Over the years, we've had a steady increase in firearm-related incidents. Some things haven't changed much. The average criminal is the same and the crazies are still crazy. The family disputes haven't changed and a drunk is still a drunk. It has been one hell of a roller coaster ride but I certainly don't miss it. Been there, done that and I've had my fill. To the future!

A walk down memory lane

Rookie Rick

Detective Rick /unmarked police car

Detective Rick

Rick and Rose

Rick and baby Jennifer

Patrol Sergeant Rick (Supervisor)

Brantford Police 125th
Anniversary Gala (April 2002)

Mark and Christine hanging out
with McGruff the Crime Dog

Jennifer sitting on police motorcycle

Rick and Mark during Police Week at the mall

Three Weddings

Jennifer and Christopher -May 12, 2018

Christine and Bradd -August 8, 2020

Trisha and Mark -August 28, 2021

Zack and Maks

Hey, put me down!

Zack gets some hugs and kisses from Mom and Dad

Maks all buckled up and ready to roll

Fur Babies

Marley (2008-2021)

Bodhi

Huck

Enjoying my time on the river

*"You can't be unhappy
in the middle of a big, beautiful river."*
- Jim Harrison

ABOUT THE AUTHOR

Retired Police Sergeant Rick DiGiandomenico was a dedicated member of the Brantford Police Service for thirty years. He was born and raised in Hamilton, Ontario, Canada. He obtained a Bachelor of Arts degree in Sociology from McMaster University in Hamilton.

He later obtained a Bachelor of Education degree and an Ontario Teachers Certificate after graduating from Brock University in St. Catharines, Ontario. After working as a classroom teacher in Hamilton, Rick decided to pursue his first love of law enforcement and was hired by the Brantford Police Force in 1985.

He worked in various sections and units that included the Uniform Patrol Section, Community Services/School Safety Section, Detective in the Youth Unit of the Criminal

Investigations Section (CIS), Sergeant in charge of the Youth Unit, Patrol Sergeant, Acting Staff Sergeant in both the Criminal Investigations and Uniform Patrol Sections, Sergeant in charge of the Court Section, Sergeant in charge of the Vice Unit in CIS and finally assigned to the Administration Branch before his retirement in 2015.

Rookie to retiree in 30 years

Police Communications/ 900 Codes

CODE	DEFINITION	CODE	DEFINITION
900	Bomb Threat	901	Homicide
902	Sudden Death	903	Attempted Suicide
904	Sex Offence	905	Indecent Act
906	Threatening	907	Assault
908	Abduction	909	Robbery
910	Extortion	911	Break & Enter
912	Theft	913	Theft-Auto
914	Possession Stolen Property	915	Fraud
916	Counterfeit Money	917	Offensive Weapon
918	Property Damage	919	Prostitution
920	Gaming and Betting	921	Drugs
922	Missing Person	923	Escapee
924	Fire	925	Theft Alarm
926	Assist Citizen	927	Assist Other Force
928	Compassionate to Locate	929	Harassing Phone Call
930	Disturbance	931	Dispute-Landlord/Tenant
931	Dispute-Landlord/Tenant	932	Dispute-Neighbor
933	Dispute-Domestic	934	Dispute-Labor
935	Intoxicated Person	936	Unwanted Person
937	Mentally Ill Person	938	Public Mischief
939	Dangerous Condition	940	Accident-Industrial
941	Accident-Farm	942	Insecure Premises
943	Property-Lost	944	Property-Found
945	Trespassing	946	Prowler
947	Suspicious Person	948	Suspicious Vehicle
949	Arrest	950	MVA-Property Damage
951	MVA-Person Injured	952	MVA-Hit and Run
953	MVA-Fatality	954	Traffic Enforcement
955	Complaint-Driving	956	Traffic Control
957	Impaired Driver	958	High Speed Chase
959	Complaint-Parking	960	Abandoned Vehicle
961	Offense-Liquor	962	Complaint-Animal
963	Complaint-Noise	964	Escort
965	Offence-Juvenile	966	Offence-Probation
967	Search Warrant	968	Offence-Shoplift
969	Injured/Sick Person	970	Missing Juvenile
971	Privately Towed Vehicle	972	Complaint-Motorcycle
973	Complaint-By-Law	974	Premise to Check
975	Paid Duty	976	Follow Up Call
977	Arrest on Warrant	978	Arson
979	Theft Under $5,000	980	Routine Detail
981	Provincial Alert	982	Zone Alert
983	Administration Notice	984	Missing Adult Located
985	Missing Juvenile Located	986	Property Returned
999	Other Admin. Details		

9-1-1 Police Dispatch Centre

Mobile Data Terminal (MDT) in police vehicle

Manufactured by Amazon.ca
Bolton, ON